Holy! Me?

The Single Adult's Guide to the Spiritual Journey

Harold Ivan Smith

Abingdon Press
Nashville

HOLY! ME?
THE SINGLE ADULT'S GUIDE TO THE SPIRITUAL JOURNEY

Copyright © 1997 by Abingdon Press

This book is printed on recycled, acid-free, elemental-chlorine-free paper.

Library of Congress Cataloging-in-Publication Data

Smith, Harold Ivan, 1947–
    Holy! Me? : the single adult's guide to the spiritual journey /
  Harold Ivan Smith.
      p.   cm.
    ISBN 0-687-01707-6 (pbk. : alk. paper)
    1. Single people—Religious life—Study and teaching.
    2. Spiritual life—Christianity—Study and teaching. I. Title.
BV4596.S5S624   1997
348.8'4—dc21

97-13507
CIP

Scripture quotations, unless otherwise noted, are from the New Revised Standard Version Bible, Copyright © 1989, by the Division of Christian Education of the National Council of the Churches of Christ in the USA. Used by permission.

Scripture quotations noted NIV are taken from the Holy Bible: New International Version. Copyright © 1973, 1978, 1984 by the International Bible Society. Used by permission of Zondervan Bible Publishers.

The prayer in section 2, note 29 by Amy Carmichael is taken from *The Gift of Prayer: A Treasury of Personal Prayer from the World's Spiritual Tradition*. Copyright © 1995. Used by permission of The Continuum Publishing Group.

The Matthew 23:37-38 citation on page 42 is from *The Inclusive New Testament*. Copyright © 1994 by Priests for Equality, Post Office Box 5243, W. Hyattsville, Md., 20782-0243.

The Luke 24:13-35 citation in section 2, note 40 is taken from *The Message: New Testament with Psalms and Proverbs* by Eugene H. Petersen. Copyright © 1993, 1994, 1995 by NavPress Publishing Group.

The prayer in section 3, note 69 entitled "The Prayer of the Chapel of the Saints and Martyrs of Our Own Time, Canterbury Cathedral" was used by permission of the authors.

The prayer in section 3, note 74 is from *A Woman's Healing Song: Prayers of Consolation for the Separated and Divorced*. Copyright 1993 by Kerrie Hide, published by Twenty-Third Publications, P.O. Box 180, Mystic, Conn., Fax 1-800-321-0411. Used by permission.

The prayers in section 3, notes 35 and 79 are from *An African Prayer Book*. Selected by Desmond Tutu. Copyright © 1995 by Desmond Tutu. Used by permission of Doubleday, a division of Bantam Doubleday Dell Publishing Group, Inc.

The passages cited in section 4, notes 9, 11, 12, and 13 are taken from "A Place to Bare Your Soul," first published in *Christian Single* (Sept. 1995). Used by permission of the author Nathan Harms.

The poem in section 4, note 53 entitled "A Thanksgiving Prayer" was written by Martha Blair. Used by permission of the author.

97 98 99 00 01 02 03 04 05 06—10 9 8 7 6 5 4 3 2 1

MANUFACTURED IN THE UNITED STATES OF AMERICA

Other Books
by
Harold Ivan Smith

Single and Feeling Good (Abingdon Press, 1987)

The Gifts of Christmas (Beacon Hill, 1989)

Singles Ask: Questions about Relationships and Sexual Issues (Augsburg, 1988)

A Time for Healing: Coming to Terms with Your Divorce (LifeWay, 1994)

51 Good Things to Do While Waiting for the Right One to Come Along (Broadman, 1995)

On Grieving the Death of a Father (Augsburg, 1995)

Death and Grief: Healing Through the Small Group (Augsburg, 1995)

Grieving the Death of a Friend (Augsburg, 1996)

To those wonderful spiritual midwives
who have nurtured and nudged me
in spiritual direction and friendship;
who have helped me explore my wonderings
and offered responses to my well-worn question,
"Holy! Me?"
The Reverend Doctor Alice Cowan
The Reverend Mary Grace Williams
Father Joe Nassal, CPPS

With gratitude

Contents

Introduction

Writing a book for single adults on spirituality is a soul-revealing task. Writing on this topic implies that someone thinks that I know how to "do" spirituality well. Reluctance takes me back to a breakfast conversation in a North Carolina inn, where travelers shared their day's destinations over eggs and hot biscuits. One guest responded to another's "How do you get there?" with "You gotta be going there to get there!" So it is with spirituality—you've got to be going there to get there!

Spirituality is not a destination to arrive at. Rather, spirituality is a journey, a lifelong pursuit, with ups and downs, detours, U-turns, blind alleys. Spirituality is not a hundred-yard dash but a marathon. Some readers may want techniques, systems, easy one-two-three's and a money-back guarantee: "This will work." The best I can offer is some guides for the journey, and some disciplines to try.

I struggle with writing this book because no one who knows me well labels me spiritual or pious. Most days, even the term pilgrim is stretching it. Seeker is probably more accurate, more comfortable, if I have to have a label. But I want you to know this: I have a deep longing to take God seriously. In the deepest canyons of my spirit, I want God's light to guide my journeying. I hunger for a Genesis-level reality: to be unashamed to be the me God intends. I hunger to be comfortable around God, to bring all of me—my particular uniqueness—to my encounter with God. I long to hear God say to me the same affirmation heard by a single adult on the banks of the Jordan two thousand years ago: "You are my beloved child, in whom I am well pleased." No, I'm not like Jesus, but I long for God's "beloved" and "well-pleased."

My friend Adele confidently counters me, "But God tells us this all day long!" Well, I can't hear for all the racket in a world obsessed with religion, in a world where many of the religious have become so obsessed with politics. With believers who insist, "If you don't believe the way I do, you're not spiritual!" Or "I won't have fellowship with you!" They always seem to have a ready litmus test. I can't hear Jesus for the loud rhetoric of angry sloganeering Christians who are more interested in their narrowly defined "family values" and political agendas than with spirituality. I am reminded of the confusion in the church when some nonbeliever friends ask, "Is Jesus like *them*?" How did religion become big business? How did Jesus get wrapped in an American flag?

Yes, all I can do, as a spiritual pilgrim, is to share my wanderings and wonderings, hoping that something I've discovered on my spiritual journey will make sense to you. Just remember: I'm not an expert or guru. I don't hang out with Mother Teresa or Billy Graham or any of the TV preachers. I am one single adult on an intense journey to a destination called wholeness, trying to make sense of a wonderful reality, a tenderly outrageous gift called Grace, modeled by a Galilean single adult who said, "I came that they may have life, and have it abundantly" (John 10:10).

Some things I will share may make you uncomfortable, because, well, some of them still make me so. I haven't had knee replacement from all the praying I've done. I am still reluctant to pray about some things. I struggle around Christians who reduce the grace to "don't-isms" and who reduce the spiritual disciplines to a bunch of daily chores. I struggle around pharisaical recruiters who are still trying to sign me up.

At times I wonder why God could offer me such a generous portion of grace and keep loving me as well. Especially when one who promised to love me stopped loving me, and as a result, I became a single adult. If she stopped loving me, couldn't God? One reality I am still learning is that God, knowing me thoroughly, loves me thoroughly. But God insists that I be honest. No hiding in the bushes as Eve and Adam did. God knows that some of my thoughts, longings, ambitions, fears, drives, are not noble or pure, admirable or excellent. He knows I stumble over, "Search me, O God . . ."

As a resident of Singleland, I have discovered that the more thoroughly people know you, the less likely they are to like you, let alone love you. Not so with God! God's thorough knowledge of me makes me more aware of God's persistent love. God devises ways so that I am not confused about that reality.

Spirituality is about responding to a gracious invitation to a kingdom headed by a single adult who always invites, "Come closer." As single adults we are graciously invited to become spiritually intimate with God and, then, with God's children. Spirituality is not a system of techniques to be practiced until mastered, but a mystery to be explored, a relationship to be experienced. Spirituality is as much an "inventure" as an adventure, and it needs lots of silence so that we can hear a God who prefers to whisper, "I love you!" Spirituality is *not* about achieving or doing but about *being*—being silent and alert, being sensitive and open, being prayerful and willing, being honest and curious, being yourself, being holy as an adult who happens to be single. Spirituality is getting comfortable with the idea of being comfortable with God. *Holy! Me?* is designed for single adults who hunger for intimacy with the God who cares for them, who know that spirituality is not a consolation prize for marriage.

Two thousand years ago a single adult named Paul rejected the spirituality of his tradition and confessed from the depths of his soul, "I want to know Christ and the power of his resurrection *and* the fellowship of sharing in his sufferings." Whew! That third desire could prove risky. It could cost a single adult everything.

There are no easy answers in this book, only my hope that someday, when you least expect it, you will be ambushed by Grace. From wherever you are at this moment, you can begin the pilgrimage. There is a time called *now*. There is a place called *here*. There is a gracious invitation to which you can answer, "Yes!"

A Note to the Reader

Ever been lost? You know the address, perhaps have a map or directions spread before you, but, alas you are lost. In this culture, many of us are "lost" about how to have a devotional life; indeed, some of us have abandoned the search for a devotional life and have settled for "having devotions"—a "two-minute" relationship with God.

Once upon a time, I thought the devotional life was simple: a little prayer, a little scripture reading and you got at the day. Sadly, I was convinced that I could find my own spiritual way. I practiced a rugged spiritual individualism. Who needs help? Not me!

Holy! Me? is not a 1-2-3 effort to turn your "two-minute" (or no-minute) spirituality into spiritual depth. This book is an invitation to make time in your life for silence, for prayer, for reading and interacting with the Scripture and sacred texts, for giving, and especially for being—for paying attention, as a single adult, to your soul.

The material has been loosely divided into five sections. Section 1 is an overview. Section 2 focuses on intentionally "being with" the Scripture and not just speed-reading. Section 3 focuses on the terrain called prayer. Section 4 explains the spiritual disciplines of journaling, paying attention, giving, making silence, and Sabbath keeping. Section 5 is a call to make space in this single season for God, for worship, for Eucharistic celebration, and for making choices that encourage spiritual depth and stability.

You do not have to read sequentially. Some readers will want to jump to units on journaling, since even a casual reading of the material will raise questions for reflection and for journaling. On the other hand, don't ignore a section because you've had a negative encounter before. As the great saint Anonymous said, "Pray as you *can*—not as you can't." And remember the object is not to "do" a discipline correctly.

It is my hope that you will look for some friends to join you in reading *Holy! Me?* Questions need to be bounced off another believer. Spiritual growth is about being part of a spiritual community, of paying attention to those spiritual hungerings. Whether in a church school class, small group, single adult fellowship, or an informal gathering over pizza, the material will be enriched by interacting with other single adults' spiritual journeys.

Remember: reading *Holy! Me?* or any book is not going to turn you into a spiritual giant overnight or into a Holy Joe or Josephine. But *Holy! Me?* is an invitation to a spiritual adventure. My goal is to encourage you to be serious about your faith, especially during this season called single. In the left-hand columns throughout the book, you're going to learn tips from single adults who were serious about their faith. Who have, in the words of our generation, "Been there, done that!" One of those, Henrietta Mears, was on target when she encouraged, "Don't waste words on the Lord. Tell him definitely what's on your mind" [*Henrietta Mears and How She Did It* (Ventura, Calif.: Regal, 1966, p. 174)].

Twenty centuries ago, a single adult encouraged his hearers to pursue a deeper life. Paul explained that spiritual hunger is God-given and that God nourishes our wonderings, "so that [single adults] would seek him and perhaps reach out for him and find him, though he is not far from each one of us" or any one of us (Acts 17:27, NIV).

Oh, in case you think that you have been disqualified for spiritual growth because of some choice you made or some life experience, consider these words of John S. Spong:

> Each of us, no matter how dark our shadows, or how condemned we are made [or have been made] to feel, are nonetheless the objects of the infinite and graceful love of God. Each of us is called to live in the wholeness of that love as one who has been embraced by the giver of infinite value. Accepting that divine valuation, we are to find the courage to be the self God has created us to be, the self we are inside the graceful gift of the righteousness of God. (*Rescuing the Bible from Fundamentalism* [San Francisco, HarperSan Francisco, 1991, p. 126])

One Old Testament writer insisted that God "devises ways so that a banished person may not remain estranged from him" (2 Samuel 14:14, NIV). In other words, God thinks up ways to stir your spiritual longings. In fact, reading this book could be part of your reconciling with the God who loves you outrageously and enthusiastically—a God who also happens to like you and who wants you to spend time with him.

The devotional life is about freedom and creativity not *shoulds* and *oughts*. I will not try to squeeze you into some mold. I offer suggestions in this book as something of a smorgasbord. Try an item, you might like it. "If Thou But Suffer God to Guide Me" is one of my favorite hymns. I sing, as have single adults for generations, "If thou but suffer God to guide thee, and hope in God through all thy ways." Well, what is the pay off? The hymn crescendos to a great promise, "God never yet forsook at need the soul that trusted God indeed" (*The United Methodist Hymnal* [Nashville: The United Methodist Publishing House, no. 142]).

I dare to believe what I sing: If I, as a single adult, trust in God to guide me, God will give [me] strength, whate'er [whatever] betide" me. And there are lots of "whatevers" in the single journey.

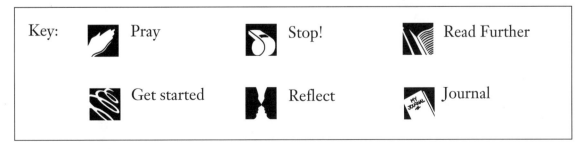

Key: Pray   Stop!   Read Further

Get started   Reflect   Journal

Holy! Me?

Section 1

1. Holy! Me? •••••••••••••••••••••••••••••••

No one in God's hall of fame was self-nominated.

"Elijah was a human being like us."
—James 5:17

Many of us are veterans of childhood Sunday school, where we had imaginative teachers who took a few liberties with the biblical text. As a result, we think of biblical heroes as bigger than life and have difficulty believing they could be relevant today. Why, they would easily conquer our spiritual challenges without working up a good sweat!

We think the label "spiritual" or "holy" fits a certain few individuals. The Pope spiritual? Yes. Mother Teresa spiritual? You bet! Billy Graham spiritual? Definitely.

Spirituality is "the engagement of the entire being in a heart-to-heart relationship with God." (Susan Muto) [1]

You may want to review the life of Elijah (see 1 Kings 17–21) a ninth-century B.C. prophet who faced extraordinary challenges. Elijah, like us, also faced lots of ordinary challenges. He spent much of his time trying to call his fellow Jews back to the intense faith of Moses and to abandoning their fascination with the gods of their neighbors. Elijah is particularly known for his correct prediction of a drought that lasted three years.

In the space below write in the names of ten people you would identify as spiritual or holy. Are you including yourself? Why or why not?

1.
2.
3.
4.
5.
6.
7.
8.
9.
10.

"Our life in the world means loving God as and where we are. Jesus did not address himself to a spiritual elite but to all who heard his voice and allowed his words to touch and change their thoughts. His teaching is full of hope for average people because he promised them they could begin again despite their failure."
(Susan Muto) [2]

 Complete this prayer:

Almighty God. You are holy. You invite me, a single adult, to be holy. Me? As a single adult, I need your help in/with for . . .

It's easy to regard certain religious figures as "spiritual giants." Ever hear the phrase, "He's no monk"? If I just lived in a monastery somewhere, *then* I could be holy. In the medieval period, some single women were told, "Get thee to a nunnery!" Isolated from the pressures and temptations of Singleland, I too might be spiritual. Guess what? Members of religious communities struggle, too. On a visit to Gethsemane Monastery in Kentucky, I was surprised—initially disappointed—when a monk explained that some days it's difficult for him to pray. "Just like you."

James's words are important for busy single adults: "Elijah was a human being *like us*." Now read it, "Elijah was a human being like . . ."

What keeps me from being comfortable with the word "holy"? What would it take for me to be holy or spiritual?

What goes through your mind when you read, "Pursue peace with everyone, and the holiness without which no one will see the Lord" (Hebrews 12:14)?

---

2. Single and Spiritually Sensitive ● ● ● ● ● ● ● ● ● ● ● ● ● ● ●

There are three types of single adults: mate-seekers, self-seekers, and kingdom-seekers.

"But strive first for the kingdom of God and his righteousness, and all these things will be given to you as well."
—*Matthew 6:33*

Single adults can be grouped into three categories: mate-seekers who are focused—even fixated—on finding the right one; self-seekers who are obsessed with themselves, first-person singular; and kingdom-seekers who focus first on noticing and then responding to their spiritual hungers. Mate-seekers think about potential spouses. Self-seekers think about needs. Kingdom-seekers think about the spirit.

At this point I would identify myself as a:

☐ Mate-seeker   ☐ Self-seeker   ☐ Kingdom-seeker

When I was first single I was a _____.

Identify friends who fit each description:

Mate-seekers	Self-seekers	Kingdom-seekers
_____	_____	_____
_____	_____	_____
_____	_____	_____

Most single adults ignore their spiritual hungers while searching for mates. But for many, particularly the newly single, singleness puts spiritual beliefs to the test. Some have been shaken to the core by a divorce or spouse's death. They are asking, "What do I—not we—believe now?" Some had a faith that was part of the "trappings" of marriage, the Sunday morning prebrunch routine. For some, the husband was the "spiritual head" of the family. "Now, how do I slip behind the driver's seat?" Moreover, in the questionings of midlife, we begin to think more about spirituality. This questioning can be troublesome for those with spiritual traditions that insist, "God had someone for you." "Oh really? Then why am I still single?"

The Big Q: What role has your faith played in your life?

_____

_____

_____

_____

_____

_____

How do your singleness and your faith influence each other?

"Lord, it is enough that you alone see and know who I am and what I am doing. It is enough that you are aware of what my life as a single person is all about." (Susan Muto) [3]

The Scripture says, "But strive *first* for the kingdom . . ." Spirituality has something essential to offer a single adult wanting to *become* the right one rather than merely to find the right one.

3. Spirituality: A Singularspective ●●●●●●●●●●●●●●●●

Spirituality invites me to bring all of me into the presence of God.

"Keep your heart with all viligance, for from it flow the springs of life."
—*Proverbs 4:23*

Just As I Am

"Just as I am, though tossed about, with many a conflict, many a doubt, fightings and fears within, without, O Lamb of God, I come! I come!" (Charlotte Elliott) [4]

Someone has said, "Religion is for those afraid of going to hell. Spirituality is for those who have already been there!" Sadly, some single adults think faith is predominantly about going to church-related activities. Many single adults go to a church because it offers ministries/programs especially for them. The idea of intimacy with God is beyond their grasp.

Although the largest potential untapped market for distributors of religion is single adults, many churches are so family-oriented that they ignore single adults. Indeed, some give the impression that the Waltons are patron saints right up there with the first-century martyrs. The theme of many churches is a nostalgic longing for some desired golden age of the family. After divorce or the death of a spouse, many no longer feel comfortable in churches they have attended for years. Never-marrieds, particularly at midlife, may detect the stirrings of a polite homophobia ("Wonder if she is a lesbian?" "Wonder if he is gay?") or condescension ("Must be psychologically impaired not to have found someone by now!").

Many single adults struggle to reconcile their sexuality with their faith, and they stay away from church until they can resolve at least some of the tension. They look for spiritual feeding here and there rather than at the community table. Such singles might think religion says, "Make yourself look presentable before you come here." Well, spirituality says, "Come as you are." That's why so many single adults have found the path to spirituality through Twelve Step programs.

What parts of you do you have to hide or ignore in order to feel accepted by your church?

_____

_____

_____

What parts of you do you have to hide or ignore in order to feel accepted or loved by God?

_____

_____

_____

Almighty God, unto whom all hearts are open, all desires known, and from whom no secrets are hid: Cleanse the thoughts of our hearts by the inspiration of thy Holy Spirit, that we may perfectly love thee, and worthily magnify thy holy Name; through Christ our Lord. Amen.[5]

"God does have a mirror in which we can see the only accurate reflection of who we are. But we will never see it as long as we carry in our minds what we have determined must be part of our lives.

"We don't approach a tangible mirror with the expectation of seeing what is not there. Yet, all too often, we do approach the mirrors of our inner selves that way." (Carole Sanderson Streeter) [6]

In the space below rewrite this prayer to include the realities of your singleness. For example, you might want to pray "from whom no sexual secrets or longings are hidden. . . ."

_____
_____
_____

How does praying so honestly/openly make you feel?
☐ very comfortable ☐ somewhat comfortable
☐ very uncomfortable ☐ confused

Why? Because _____
_____
_____

4. Spirituality Is More Than Systems and Techniques • •

Techniques and systems sabotage healthy spiritual growth.

"I can will what is right, but I cannot do it." —Romans 7:18

Paul: A Single's Testimony
" . . . I have belonged to the strictest sect of our religion and I lived as a Pharisee" (Acts 26:5).

These helpful words were written by a single adult, Paul. You would think the guy who wrote one-third of the New Testament would have had spirituality down pat. Before his conversion, Paul knew all the techniques and was rather prideful about his zealous religious practices. Some single adults still imitate Paul's approach.

In the box trace your thumb. If you have an ink stamp pad, place your thumb on the pad to leave a thumbprint in the box below the words: "No one in the world has a thumbprint like mine."

"Even though I, too, have reason for confidence in the flesh. If anyone else has reason to be confident in the flesh, I have more: circumcised on the eighth day, a member of the people of Israel, of the tribe of Benjamin, a Hebrew born of Hebrews; as to the law, a Pharisee; as to zeal, a persecutor of the church; as to righteousness under the law, blameless. Yet whatever gains I had, these I have come to regard as loss because of Christ."—*Philippians 3:4-7*

"Most of life occurs in the ditches and trenches of pedestrian routine. It is here that we must respond to the Lord's call if we are to find the real meaning of an everyday spirituality lived in the world and not inflict on ourselves an unrealistic model based on someone else's gifts."
(Susan Muto) [7]

If your thumbprint is that unique, why should your devotional life mimic another's? God doesn't make spiritual clones or twins. To have a devotional life, you only have to be yourself.

After my divorce I thought I was forever destined to a second-class spiritual life. Why would God want an intimate relationship with a "blemished" individual? But I did try hard to do spirituality. If someone said, "This is the way to be spiritual" I was willing to give it a go. Now I know to be cautious of people who say or teach, "Here's the system: one, two, three," to be cautious of anyone who promises surefire but effortless results from a particular technique. Spirituality cannot be reduced to a formula: so many parts prayer to so many parts Bible reading and presto! Now you're spiritual!

> *One reason many single adults are looking for a new system or technique is*
> _____
> _____.

Or possibly because the last system or technique didn't work. Paul walked away from reliance on a system when he encountered Jesus. Paul discovered that he had been invited into a relationship not into a system of rigid religious practices. All single adults need to make the same discovery.

> *Who is offering you advice on mastering "the system"?*
> _____
>
> *What troubles or annoys you about their suggestion?*
> _____
> _____

Take a moment to reflect on Paul's words in this section. Is there some liberty in them for you?

> *Write a "thank-you" note to Paul.*
> _____
> _____

5. Spirituality Is Not Reserved for Marrieds! •••••••

If there are no fruits of the Spirit in my life now there will be none when/if I marry.

"There was also a prophet, Anna . . . a widow . . . She never left the temple but worshiped there with fasting and prayer night and day."
—Luke 2:36, 37

"I had to talk to God. I had no one else to talk to. My own daughter didn't speak to me for five years after she went to live with her mother." —Michael

"I always thought going to church was enough . . . until the divorce. No one would ever have accused me of being a 'holy roller.' Then I got humbled." —Karen

"I discovered I had no faith of my own. All those years I was married, I hung on to my husband's spiritual coattails. I was taught that he was supposed to be the spiritual head of the family. I never had any religious thoughts of my own. His death devastated me spiritually."
—Elaine

"Well, the truth is that I had a little feud with the Lord. I heard ministers say that God would give me the desires of my heart. Well, when I hit the big 4-0, I said, 'Okay, God, where's mine if you love me so much?' Yes, I prayed in some tight jams, but that was about it. I mean, what was so wrong with wanting to be married and having kids? Why can't I have the great American dream, too?" —Becky

Okay, I'll admit it. Some spirituality or deeper-life-type books drive me to distraction, especially when the examples are geared toward "the couple that prays together, stays together" and when some promise better sex. It's like a fantasy to be colored with crayons. Married couples pray together and then—none of that tossing-and-turning-can't-get-to-sleep business single adults know about.

Yet, people who have studied the spiritual devotional habits of marrieds say it's not so hot. A few verses out of the devotional book, a prayer, and then—I was surprised to learn that a lot of people do not regularly pray with their spouses. Indeed, I was stunned by one minister who said that his wife's rather simplistic prayers distracted him from praying.

It's one of those things the inner critic tells us: "If only we were married, then we could be part of a dynamic spiritual duo. Certainly, some single-agains do miss that spiritual intimacy they had in a marriage. But others regret that spirituality was not part of their marriage. "I always felt," Joan confessed, "that something was missing. I mean, we went to church but . . ."

Some adults begin the search for spirituality only after a marriage ends. "I had to turn to God," Bill said, "to keep my sanity as a single parent of three teens."

> **M** *Which one of the testimonies in the left column resembles your pilgrimage? How did you recognize your need for faith?*
>
> _____
>
> _____

Yes, it is hard to imagine that Anna was for real. I mean "day and night"? Isn't that a little too much? But then, Anna was old. I interpret this scripture to mean that Anna incorporated her faith into all of her life. Faith was more than a one-day-a-week experience for her. She lived out her single season with all of herself open to God.

Ironically, in the Christmas pageants and cards, songs, and stories, we overlook that just as God included shepherds, wise men, a cash-hungry innkeeper, and a paranoid king in the script, God also deliberately included a single adult, Anna.

Investing yourself into your faith might well prepare you to become the right one for someone. It might also prepare you to be sensitive to the spiritual priorities of those you date and especially those you would consider "prime" matrimonial prospects. But, even more, it does wonders in helping you mature as a believer.

6. Spirituality Is More Than a Buzzword • • • • • • • • • • •

Buzzwords are like icebergs: 10 percent visible, 90 percent below the surface.

"Now all the Athenians . . . spend their time in nothing but telling or hearing something new."
—Acts 17:21

What comes to mind when you hear these words?

Spirituality _____

Religion _____

Faith _____

Church _____

Single adults love the "latest." Even words and phrases come and go. Vocabulary today is definitely faddish. Ever go out with a vocabulary-time-warped adult? The third *groovy* can quickly dispel any romantic potential. When a new term, word, or phrase appears, because of our technological communications capacities that phrase is everywhere: consider nanosecond.

Think of our computer-generated language. List words that would have been alien in your childhood. Some examples include: fax, E-mail, and compact disc.

_____   _____   _____

_____   _____   _____

_____   _____   _____

Do you remember when you first heard the phrase "Higher Power"? What do you think when you hear the phrase now?

_____

_____

The issue becomes more complicated because of our reliance on theology, doctrine, and dogma. For example, what do the words of the Apostles' or Nicene Creed mean to you? Early nineteenth-century Southern evangelist Sam Jones used to compare theology and botany. "I don't know much about botany but I love flowers." Many single adults would admit, "I know little about theology but I do love God and know God loves me." But it is not uncommon for single adults with spiritual-based longings and questions to be uncomfortable with the prepackaged answers the church and many religious authorities are offering.

Sadly, other single adults are quick to label anything spiritual as "New Age" or to view any fresh approach as questionable. Yet the reality is that God is revealed in the Scripture as a God who seeks us. "So that they would search for God and perhaps grope for him and find him—though indeed he is not far from each of us" (Acts 17:27).

We need to pay attention to our spiritual longings, especially as we begin to sense our spiritual emptiness. Especially as the "newest, latest, biggest, best" somehow don't satisfy us. Athenians spent their time talking and listening to the religious opinions and experiences of others. If we neglect the spiritual dimension of our lives, we will be impoverished in every other dimension.

What three questions express your longings for a vital faith?

1. _____

2. _____

3. _____

---

7. Spirituality "On the Run" Is Not Spirituality • • • • • • •

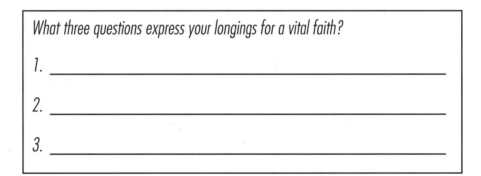

We live in a culture that is schedule-centric. Yet, why settle for a "one-minute" faith?

"They will accumulate for themselves teachers to suit their own desires. . . ."—*2 Timothy 4:3*

"These are the times that try men's souls." Thomas Paine said these words during the American Revolution struggle. Yet, they are still so current—perhaps all we need to do is add an exclamation point! If only we had the spiritual equivalent of the Environmental Protection Agency for the soul. Contemporary American culture is not soul-friendly. A rampant materialism tag teamed with a frantic obsession for success leaves us with little quality time to think about the eternal.

So many single adults settle for spiritual junk food. Then they tip their hats at God: "Love to talk to you, but I've got to run." Places to go, people to see, deals to make—that's life in the fast lane in Singleland. Too many of us are caught up in the Daytimer, check-off-on-the-checklist society.

> *Stop reading. How many items are on your have-to-be-done-today list? Do you feel guilty taking time to read this, time you could be spending on tasks to be checked off? Which—if any—of those items have lasting significance?*
>
> _____
>
> _____
>
> _____
>
> *How many items are like impatient schoolchildren waving their hands for a teacher's recognition? Me!! How many tire your soul rather than nourish it? How many don't need to be done at all?*
>
> _____
>
> _____
>
> _____
>
> *Who is in control of your life?*
> ☐ *the to-do-today list*   ☐ *me*
> ☐ *others*   ☐ *my employer*
> ☐ *my children*   ☐ *my ex-spouse*
> ☐ _____
>
> *Would you panic if you lost your list?* _____

Maybe that's why a lot of single adults have "potty" devotionals. I had dinner with a former editor of *Reader's Digest* who told me the ultimate explanation for the popularity of that magazine: an article could be read in one bathroom sitting. There are hundreds of daily devotional books on the market. Such prepackaged spiritual food reminds me of those instant soup kits—all I have to do is pour in a cup of hot water and stir. "A delicious meal, almost as good as Mom's," it says on the package. Circle the key words: almost as good as. . . .

So many single adults are like me standing in front of one of those healthy-snack vendors in airports. I have no time for a meal and no stomach for another delicious airline culinary memory. No. "I'll have a quarter pound of the yogurt almonds, please." I gobble most of them down before I even get on the plane. Well, yes, it was a between-meal snack but it was yogurt almonds (healthier, right?)

and I ate them standing up (definitely fewer calories than sitting down) and my selection was definitely better than one of those airport hot dogs!

How many times have you and I decided to eat "better"? To lay off the meal-in-a-bag-in-the-drive-through, to eat healthy and avoid the deep-frieds? And how many times have we decided to "eat" heathily spiritually? We keep telling ourselves that spirituality on the run is "just as good but less demanding." But most of our agendas, in an era that tries our souls, leave us walking around with malnourished souls. We're engaging in single parenting with malnourished souls. Systems and techniques seductively appeal to us. They enable us to calm our longings, to ease our guilt. "Well, it's better than nothing. . . ." or "This will work!" Yet the words are hardly out of our mouths before we are internally doubting.

8. Making Time for Spirituality •••••••••••••••••••

It does take time to be holy.

"Give thanks in all circumstances."
—1 Thessalonians 5:18

The most common expression in America—especially in the case of single parents—has to be, "Would love to . . . but I don't have time." Are you as amused as I am by those gigantic Daytimers people lug around? We are a generation addicted to anything labeled "timesaving."

> Look at our time-oriented vocabulary: microwave, quick-stop, fast lane, and permapress. Can you think of other examples?
>
> _____   _____   _____
>
> _____   _____   _____
>
> _____   _____   _____

Shaving off a minute or two here adds up. A minute saved is a minute earned. Doing two things at once saves time—driving and talking on the cellular or driving and eating. I have been amused and frustrated by churches that want only an eighteen-minute sermon; three points and a poem. I am sometimes given a time-sequence of the service—hymn: four minutes and thirty seconds, prayer: two minutes. It sounds like express-lane worship.

There used to be a popular hymn, "Take Time to Be Holy" in all Protestant hymnals. Now the hymn is embarrassingly oxymoronic, a relic to a bygone era. But every so often I hum a few bars:

Take time to be holy, speak oft with thy Lord; abide in Him
   always, and feed on his word.
Make friends of God's children, help those who are weak,
Forgetting in nothing his blessing to seek.[8]

The second verse is annoying: "Take time to be holy, the world rushes on. . . ." No wonder the hymn has been dropped by some hymnal publishers. We don't go to church to be nettled by archaic words—especially not in a culture that loves anything beginning with, "One Minute."

On the run? Maybe that's why Cat Stevens's hit song "Cat's in the Cradle," about a father who's too busy for his son, is still getting airtime.

> Do we manage time or does time manage us? How would you answer that question?
>
> "How is it that people today, with ever-more refined instruments for measuring milliseconds, seconds, minutes, hours, and days, complain that they have no time to get anything done?" (Susan Muto) [9]

> List some timesaving devices you have that your grandparents did not have.
>
> _____   _____
> _____   _____
> _____   _____

I am told that "I don't have time" was never part of my grandmother's vocabulary.

How many times have you lovingly told someone, "If you don't slow down, you're . . ."? Yet, do we ever say lovingly, "If you don't slow down and take time for your soul . . ."?

> I have had many people in my seminars protest, "But I don't have time to meditate, to pray, to read scripture." What I want to say is, "You don't have time NOT to pray!"

Some of these same people have time for jogging, or racquetball, or socializing over a coffee. Why? Because they make time. As single adults, we make time for what we value.

It's not easy for me to get up, meditate, and then jog, but both activities are time well spent. Both are an investment, if you will, in my spiritual and physical health. Some time in my day has to be carved out—and protected from competing priorities—for nourishing my soul.

> What is nonnegotiable in your daily routine?
> 1. _____
> 2. _____
> 3. _____
> 4. _____
> 5. _____
>
> When is best for you to have soul time?
>
> _____
>
> What would you have to do to make time for soul nourishing?
> I would have to _____.
> I could   _____.
> Or I could   _____.

9. Spirituality Is Being, Not Doing! • • • • • • • • • • • • • •

> Spirituality is not something you do—it is something you are.

> "You shall love the Lord your God with all your heart, and with all your soul, and with all your mind." —Matthew 22:37

I will never forget the frigid winter day I had a soul-warming moment while reading. I have forgotten the author but not her words: "We are human *beings* not human *doings*." That was a freeing discovery and a big step for me in befriending spirituality, in shedding the lingering guilt of a system of do this and this and this. That day I was freed from guilt-driven devotions.

As long as you see spirituality as things you do, you miss the intimacy of a relationship. People who love each other want to spend time together. Yet, most men have difficulty with being-centric relationships. After a few minutes we say, "Let's go *do* something. . . ." Maybe that's why we have trouble with our spiritual dimensions.

Spirituality is not about *doing* spiritual exercises in a correct manner or method. Spirituality is about *being*. It is about being surprisable—say by a sunrise or cloud formation. It is about being interruptible—by a sense of wonder for God's grace or a stunning sunset. It is about noticing—the intricacies of nature all around us that God deliberately crafted like an unusual rock formation. It is about being aware and alert to the moment—this particular moment at this particular place. It is about being grateful—for a relationship with God and an awareness that God knows my name is Harold Ivan. It is about being me—the unique individual God designed me to be. It is about being alert to what God is up to these days in my life and my community.

> Spirituality is about being—not doing.

There are mornings I do not read twelve verses of scripture. There are mornings I do not say twelve words in prayer. There are mornings I do not sing my favorite hymns. Once that would have been enough for me to indict myself as a spiritual weakling, because I then thought spirituality was a checklist of items to be done correctly.

But these days I have discovered a spirituality that allows me to be with God on my back deck. I am comfortable with God rocking awhile before dawn in the silence of a home in which there is only one resident. I enjoy a spirituality that sees sacredness in the playfulness of two squirrels; a spirituality that sees wonderment at the great windows of Chartres Cathedral; a spirituality that brings me, openmouthed, heart-beating into the presence of Michelangelo's *David*. Perhaps other tourists only saw a twelve-foot marble man. I saw the telltale fingerprints of God who gifted a single adult with the skill to sculpt something so stunning.

Perhaps a whole new way of being yourself with God awaits you too.

Name some places you have discovered God.

1. _____

2. _____

3. _____

4. _____

5. _____

Section 2

10. Taking Scripture Intentionally • • • • • • • • • • • • • •

INVENTORY: Put a check beside each statement that captures your experience in reading the Scripture.

- [ ] My mind wanders when I read the Bible.
- [ ] I don't have time to read the Bible.
- [ ] I have a hard time understanding the Bible especially _____.
- [ ] Most of my single friends read the Bible more than I do.
- [ ] I read the Bible in spurts.

The Bible is a marvelous treasury for spiritual growth.

"But their delight is in the law of the LORD, and on his law they meditate day and night."
—*Psalm 1:2*

The story is told of a young hearing-impaired girl who insisted that Santa Claus was not real and that she could prove it. So, as she waited in line, she confidently rehearsed her plan to debunk the jolly red-clad man's reputation.

When it was her turn to sit on Santa's lap, he beckoned to her to come. She turned to her mother and signed, "Watch this!" Santa saw her signing and when she was firmly settled on his lap, he signed to her, "How are you, today?" and called her by name (he had seen her mother sign her name). She was stunned! If Santa could communicate with her by signing, he had to be real!

God has chosen to speak to us through his Son and through his Word, the Bible. God inspired a wide variety of human authors to compose the Bible. God still actively speaks to single adults through the Bible. Yet many single adults read the Bible very haphazardly. But God, like the Santa in this story, wants to communicate his love to us!

"It is the Bible's primary message that only in decision for God and acceptance of His grace at the cost of faithful obedience to His will is our salvation. And this cannot be put off indefinitely; *now* is the time." (Georgia Harkness) [1]

The central theme of the Scripture was captured in a children's song written by Anna Warner, a single adult who led Bible studies for cadets at West Point:

Jesus loves me! This I know, for the Bible tells me so. [Single adults] to him belong; they are weak, but he is strong.

"For the Bible tells me so" are words I need to sing on days when it is hard to believe that I am loved. Maybe that's why Anna repeated the phrase three times, "Yes, Jesus loves me." [2]

Some of us have been beaten over the head by the Bible—or more accurately by selected interpretations of scriptural texts. This is especially true on the issue of divorce. "God hates divorce" some snarl, citing chapter and verse, and their tone of voice implies that God hates divorced people as well. Or, they delve into the Scripture to prove their reasoning of why the divorced cannot remarry. Sadly, their positions are often entrenched, especially when they declare, "*My* Bible says. . . ." The Bible is too commonly used to prop up ideas, notions, and beliefs, a technique called "proof texting."

Some of us simply do not understand the Bible. We know we should read it. We may even want to. We believe other single adults read the Scripture more frequently or with more understanding than we do. But, as one person protested, "It's so difficult to understand!" If God expected us to read it, why didn't he make it plainer?

What keeps you from reading the Scripture?

_____

_____

_____

Henrietta Mears, a single adult who pioneered much of what we know of Christian education, used to answer that question from single adults with a counterquestion: "If God knew we would need coal, why did he bury it so deep in the earth?" [3] Her book, *What the Bible Is All About* (Regal Books) is a fine tool for the single adult who wants to better understand the Bible.

"A method of some kind is essential. It is not enough to keep reading our favorite passages. Nor should we imitate the butterfly and flit irresponsibly from verse to verse."
(John Stott) [4]

Sometimes the problem is that a particular translation is not reader-friendly. Fortunately, we live in a time when reader-friendly translations are readily available.

Sometimes the problem is the way we read the Bible. We do not give it a chance. Just before going to bed, we reach—perhaps grudgingly—for the Bible and scan a few verses or chapters, hoping to stave off the guilt engendered by some leaders: "Real Christians read the Bible every day!" We nibble on appetizers and think that will nourish us spiritually.

Sometimes the problem is that we don't want the Bible to challenge our behaviors, our ideas, or our attitudes.

"Don't ever suppose reading little scraps can ever be compensation for doing deep and consecutive work on the Bible itself."
(Henrietta Mears) [5]

"There is not much point in reading the Bible at all if we never put it into practice. To pray, think, and remember are wasted effort if we then reject what we have learned."
(John Stott) [6]

James Bryant Smith, who has a real sensitivity to single adults and the Bible, reminds us:

"The Holy Spirit opens our minds when we read the Bible, making us receptive to its message. In particular, the Spirit helps us to read the passage for what it is saying to us personally, applying its message to our particular situation.

Sit down with your Bible and select a passage to reflect upon. As you read, pray that the Holy Spirit will highlight a particular verse or word that is specifically meant for you to hear."[7]

A Prayer of Invitation to the Holy Spirit

Holy Spirit this seems strange to me.
Never before have I invited you to be with me as I read the Scripture.
Guide my reading.
Open my eyes to God's Word for me.
Help me not be distracted.
Calm my impatience.
Feed my spiritual hunger.
As I read this passage, God, what do you want me to see?

Steve Harper has formulated some questions single adults should consider. Be prayerful as you answer them.

Yes	No	?	
☐	☐	☐	Am I reading the Bible in a way that brings me in contact with the whole of it?
☐	☐	☐	Do I read the Scripture in large enough portions to see isolated passages in their larger contexts?
☐	☐	☐	Do I use responsible tools to add the insights of others to my own study?
☐	☐	☐	Do I have any means of marking, noting, and recording my discoveries?[8]

I would add three more questions:

☐	☐	☐	Am I intentional about reading the Scripture?
☐	☐	☐	Do I make time in my day to read?
☐	☐	☐	Do I rely on others to interpret the Bible for me?

Notice that I did not ask how many scriptures you read. I realize some single adults are under the impression that they should be reading the Bible through consecutively, "from cover to cover," as my grandfather used to say, meaning from Genesis to the Revelation. Some traditions imply this is proof of an individual's spirituality. For some single adults, this has become a source of false spiritual pride. Harper commented on the reading habits of John Wesley, founder of the Methodist Church, who spent much of his life as a single adult: "He knew that he had a lifetime to read the Bible, so he did not have to hurry."[9]

Why should you dash through the Scripture, gobbling down spiritual food as if in a fast-food establishment? Savor. Enjoy! And like Crackerjacks, look for the gifts inside!

Henrietta Mears faced the problem of being turned into a spiritual "expert" during her many years teaching single adults at First Presbyterian Church in Hollywood, California. The question, she reminded her single adults, is not, "What does Miss Mears say, *but* what does the Bible say!" [10]

Today, with the growth of "Bible teaching" ministries, particularly through radio, television, books, and tapes, many single adults are using the equivalent of *Cliff Notes:* "Dr. So-and-So says . . ."

Soon, Dr. So-and-So does their thinking for them. Some single adults respond, "Well, he was trained in a seminary," or "She reads the Greek," or "He's so well respected." That may be so. But it cannot take the place of your reading the Bible for yourself.

Take a moment to reflect on this question: Who is my authority on the Bible? Who tells me what the Bible says or means?

_____

_____

_____

God, you know my experience in reading the Bible. After reading this material, I want to say to you

_____

_____

_____.

Take a moment to review your daily schedule. Is there some time you could prioritize for Bible reading? The amount of time is not important. Schedule an appointment with yourself. I could read at _____ for _____ minutes.

11. Reading the Bible Seriously ● ● ● ● ● ● ● ● ● ● ● ● ● ●

The Bible deserves to be taken seriously.

"And how from childhood you have known the sacred writings that are able to instruct you for salvation through faith in Christ Jesus."
—2 Timothy 3:15

If someone were to ask you, "Do you take the Bible seriously?" how would you answer?
I take the Bible seriously by _____.
I take the Bible seriously by _____.
I take the Bible seriously by _____.

To ensure that his Bible study times were unhurried, Wesley chose the early hours of the morning and the quiet hours of the evening. These times allowed him the space to meditate on what he read. His main goal was quality, not quantity. Wesley normally read at least a chapter per sitting, but sometimes he would read only a few verses. His desire was to encounter God, and when he did that, the amount he read was not the most important thing.[11]

One way we take the Bible seriously is by *making* the time to read. There may be moments when we are so stressed or hurried that our reading is perfunctory. At times, it may be best to wait a while to read. On the other hand, scripture can literally "leap out" at us in such moments. Steve Harper offers some helpful insights based on the spiritual habits of John Wesley.

> Reread the paragraph about Wesley and underline the phrases that capture your attention. Did anything challenge you? What is your goal in reading the Bible?

I hope you noted "quality not quantity." That may be one of the best gifts we can discover in Wesley's life.

"Five lines or five pages—what does it matter as long as I am present to what I read?"
(Susan Muto) [12]

"Quality time" is enhanced by inviting God to be with us in reading the Scripture. We take a pretty casual approach probably because of the availability of Bibles. However, I was stunned when I visited China at how few Chinese single adults actually own a Bible. The tendency for many in America is to grab and skim until we find something to read, probably an old favorite verse or a psalm, perhaps something we have known from our childhood.

"Proper reading of Scripture is not a technical exercise that can be learned; it is something that grows or diminishes according to one's own spiritual frame of mind."
(Dietrich Bonhoeffer) [13]

What would happen if you followed this approach to reading the Bible?

1. Find a comfortable, quiet place to read, free from distractions.

2. Sit quietly for a moment, breathe some deep breaths, let your soul catch up with your body.

3. Pray: "God, I invite you to be present with me while I read this your Word. Speak to me in a way that will be easy for me to understand and that will remind me of your love for me."

"If I read the Bible in a scientifically theological or scholarly way, it does not make me happy. But if I read in it that God so loved the world, . . . then I am happy! (Corrie ten Boom) [14]

4. Begin reading. Pause occasionally to let the words or thoughts sink in. Remember: the goal is quality not quantity.

5. Reread the passage. Try to sum up that passage in your own words. Look for key words. Pause in silence for a moment.

6. Thank the Lord for giving the Bible and for the time to reflect on its application to your life. Ask God to bring that which you have read back to mind through the day or night.

"Since the Bible is God's Word, we cannot read it with the casual indifference which we might give to the daily newspaper. . . . We shall also cry out to the Holy Spirit to illumine our minds, and in particular to show Christ to us. The Holy Spirit delights, in answer to our prayers, to bring Jesus Christ alive in our Bible reading. Thus, echoing the Emmaus disciples, we too will be able to testify that our hearts were 'burning within us while he . . . opened the Scriptures to us.' "—(Luke 24:32) [15]

As you read and study the Scripture pray: "In this particular passage, O Lord, is there a warning light for me? Is there guidance for an issue I will soon be facing? Is there some fresh insight into your character and mercy?"

12. Reading Formationally • • • • • • • • • • • • • • • • • • •

The Bible is to be read with our hearts as well as with our eyes and brains.

"Do you understand what you are reading?" —Acts 8:30

When Henrietta Mears was a young reader, her mother would come up to her, take the book from Henrietta and demand, "What does it say?" Sometimes, Henrietta would respond, "Mother, I've only been reading ten minutes," to which Mother Mears would respond, "If you have been reading that long, you certainly should have learned something. Now tell me what you have read." [16]

It is possible to read the Scripture and yet not have it speak to us.

"Instead of aggressively manipulating the text to suit my needs, I simply let it speak." (Susan Muto) [17]

Much has been made of right-brain and left-brain thinking. In a sense, those realities play into how we read the Scripture. Whatever our approach, we can be shaped by reading the Scripture, or it can be just another item on the day's list of "things to do."

"Formative reading could thus be defined as the art of listening with inner ears of faith to what God is saying in the happenings which comprise our life." (Susan Muto) [18]

Dr. Robert Mulholland suggests that Christians tend to read "informationally" rather than "formationally." Mulholland compares the two reading styles. After reading them try to decide which style you use when you read.

INFORMATIONAL READING	FORMATIONAL READING
Seeks to cover as much of the text as possible.	Object is not to cover as much as possible; slower reading is preferred.
Linear—chapter two follows chapter one; Exodus follows Genesis.	In depth—look for multiple layers of meaning.
Reader seeks to "master" the text, often in order to justify personal interpretations.	Text masters the reader.
Text is there for the reader to control/ manipulate according to his/her purposes.	Text becomes the subject of a relationship; the reader is the object "shaped" by the text.
Reader is analytical, critical, and judgmental. We read through the filters of our own desires, perceptions, wants, and needs.	Reader is humble, detached, willing, loving approach: "Lord, speak…"
Based on a problem-solving mentality.	Open to the mystery of the text.
Requires no preparation. Just start reading.[19]	Requires spiritual preparation.

The Bible is not to be read to collect data for some equivalent of spiritual trivial pursuit.

My single adult friend Carole reminds me that there is a time and place for both styles, even a mysterious blend of the two approaches. Some have begun reading to respond to a question or issue in their lives and then—without really noticing—switched into a formational reading style. The goal is to read, reflect, and apply.

I have a series of questions I use in interacting with the Scripture.

1. In this particular passage, O Lord, is there a warning light for me?
2. Is there guidance for an issue I am facing?
3. Is there fresh insight into your character? Or into your compassion?
4. Is there something that will disturb my spiritual "point of view"?
5. Is this passage an anvil on which I need to lay my soul?

But, you ask, what about those passages that are hard to understand—like those prophecies or genealogies? Whew!

"If when you come across something in Scriptures that in your limited knowledge you do not understand just then, lay the item aside temporarily and go on. Later in your study, and in spiritual maturity, you will find the solution."
(Henrietta Mears) [20]

Someone accurately summarized the goal by saying that God holds us responsible for the portions we understand, not the portions we do not understand.

"As we honor Him by appreciating the beauty of His handiwork in nature, so we honor Him by learning to appreciate the beauty and the richness of the form of the Holy Scriptures."
(Bertha Munro) [21]

I have grown up loving many of the great hymns of the church, some of which were written by a single adult, Isaac Watts. Two centuries after his death, some of the 700 hymns he composed are still popular: "When I Survey the Wondrous Cross," "Alas and Did my Savior Bleed?" "We're Marching to Zion," and the legendary, "O God Our Help in Ages Past." In reading Watts's biography I learned that he didn't just thumb through the book of Psalms looking for something to turn into a hymn. Rather, the Psalms had become such a part of his spirituality because he had read them formationally, from childhood. Take his "O God Our Help in Ages Past" and lay it beside Psalm 90 and the inspiration for the hymn becomes obvious. Isaac Watts read the Psalms to be shaped by them.

Marking is a means of shorthand.

When the Ethiopian single adult was asked by Philip if he understood what he was reading from the book of Isaiah, he responded, "How can I unless someone guides me?"—*Acts 8:31*

This verse of scripture reminds me that sometimes single adults read and struggle with scriptures they do not understand. God will bring someone, in time, into their life to help them comprehend.

I used to worry about what would happen to my books after my death, because of my habit of marking what I read. I underline. I write in the margins. A library will never be interested in my large collection of books because one could tell that the books have been read and "used." But then books are the resources for not only my writing but also for my faith. I also write and mark my Bibles.

My friend Charlie Shedd helped me adapt one of the most practical ways to mark, to supplement the underlining in reading the Bible. Charlie suggested writing these marks in the margins by verses:

Heart—I like this.

Q or ?—I don't understand this.

Arrow—This gets me!

I have expanded Charlie's system with these marks:

—This really applies to single adults.

Nail—This "nails" me.

+—This helps me.

Clockface—I need to spend some time with this.

I have found it helpful to write dates beside some verses, particularly those that collided with my reality on a particular date. It has been amazing to go back through a particular Bible and let the dates remind me of special situations. I cannot always remember the specifics of the situation, but the dates tell me that God met me through reading that particular verse. This gives me confidence that God will meet me again. Remember the old comedian gimmick: a man gets slapped in the face and responds, "Thanks, I needed that!" The Scripture can have the same impact and lead us to confess, "I needed that!"

> "Rigid, doctrinaire believers who seem to confuse grace with morals have accused me and others of following a sentimental, do-gooder, soft God of love. . . . These critical Christians who label me as too liberal and more centered on God's love than on His judgment have not seen my marked-up Bible."
> (Eugenia Price) [22]

Some single adults have a fear of marking scriptures. Some have been wrongly taught that marking shows disrespect for the Bible. The Bible is meant to be read and to be a resource not an idol to be worshiped! Marking is a way to enhance the learning.

14. Reading Various Translations • • • • • • • • • • • • • •

> Scripture comes alive when it is read in various translations.
>
> "I will not forget your word."—*Psalm 119:16*

Thirty years ago, scripture reading was pretty much in the King James Version. Today there are over 100 versions of Bibles available and more in development. The choices can be bewildering.

> "Seek and ye shall find, the right translation."
> (Bill Wolfe) [23]

But how do I select a version that will be a good one for me?

☐ Do a test read in a bookstore. Take a favorite text, such as John 3:16 or Psalm 23, read and compare the translations.

☐ Check out not only the translation but also the added features. Many of the differences are in the "special helps" section.

☐ Does a particular translation "read" comfortably?

☐ Do you want this Bible for personal Bible study? Small group work? Show?

☐ Look at the type size and amount of white space on a page. Consider a single column rather than the double column, because of the larger print.

☐ Feel the paper texture—will a highlighter bleed through? Hold the paper up to the light; you should not be able to see through.

☐ Examine the Study Helps such as concordance, maps, cross-references, charts, and commentaries. How much of this will you regularly use? Check out the concordance—the way to find verses using key words.

A Guide to Some Common Translations

- ☐ *King James 1611*—Poetic, reflects Elizabethan English; traditional. Reading level about twelfth grade.

- ☐ *New King James 1991*—Preserves much of flavor of original KJV but in updated language. Reading level about seventh grade.

- ☐ *New International Version 1978*—Popular with evangelical, conservative Christians. Reading level about sixth grade.

- ☐ *New Revised Standard 1995*—Update of Revised Version. Uses gender-inclusive language so that Psalm 32:1 is "Happy are those" rather than "Blessed is he . . ." Reading level about seventh grade.

- ☐ *Contemporary English 1991*—Uncomplicated English. Very helpful for new Bible readers and young people. Reading level about fourth grade.

- ☐ *Today's English 1976*—Also called Good News Bible. Substitutes modern phrases and language. Reading level about sixth grade.

- ☐ *New American Standard 1971*—Revision of 1901 American Standard Version. Reading level about ninth grade.

- ☐ *The Living Bible 1971*—A paraphrase. Reading level about seventh grade.

- ☐ *The Message 1993*—Contemporary language paraphrase. Reading level, data not available.

☐ Consider a parallel version that features translations side-by-side on a page for comparison.

☐ Consider the price but remember, a Bible is an investment.

☐ Ask friends what they like/dislike about their particular translations. Listen, but don't let someone select your Bible for you.

I read different translations of the New Testament. During my study of Corrie ten Boom for writing about her in *Movers and Shapers*, I discovered that she read the Phillips translation. So I purchased a paperback copy and read it for a year. The next year I read the Williams translation of the New Testament. When *The Message* first came out I read that.

Currently I am reading the more radical *Inclusive New Testament*, which is helping me, as a male, become more sensitive to the exclusive language I often use even without thinking. For example, consider this verse, "In the resurrection, people don't marry at all—they are like God's angels. But on the subject of the resurrection, haven't you read what God told you 'I am the God of Abraham and Sarah, the God of Isaac and Rebecca, the God of Jacob and Rachel and Leah!'" [24]

I find it creatively helpful to read passages aloud. My friend, Audrey Williamson, a widow in her eighties, said one benefit of living alone was that she could pray and read the Scripture aloud in the middle of the night with no worry of disturbing anyone. Audrey turned Bible reading into an art form. Henrietta Mears recognized that much of her lifelong love of the Scripture and the career of teaching Christian education was shaped by hearing her mother read the Bible aloud.

"So Pharaoh called his ministers together again and said, 'This won't do. We shall soon be completely overrun by Israelites, so I've hit upon the idea of throwing all their baby boys into the river Nile. How does that strike you?' 'Oh, what a superb scheme,' said the ministers. Pharaoh hastened to implement his plan, and presumably the Nile crocodiles approved of this change in breakfast food."
(Rosemary Lea) [25]

I thoroughly enjoyed *Miss Lea's Bible Stories for Children* (Zagat Survey), which imaginatively brings Bible stories to life. This would be a great resource for single parents. Consider the example in the margin.

 On Buying a New Bible

So how does one go about getting a new Bible? Hint that for a birthday or Christmas, you would appreciate a gift certificate to a bookstore with a large Bible selection. If you want more than one translation, consider buying a used book and having the Bible re-covered.

15. Sensing the Feminine Voice in Scripture • • • • • • • •

I have to read what is there—not what I want to be there.

"And those who ate were about five thousand men, besides women and children."
—*Matthew 14:21*

"My endeavor is to bring out of Scripture what is there, and not to thrust in what I think might be there." (Charles Simeon) [26]

Historically the Bible was pretty much the domain of males. After all, they interpreted, translated, taught, and preached the Scripture. To say the least, the treatment of women was rarely favorable, particularly in the Old Testament with characters like Eve, Jezebel, and Delilah composing a trinity of seduction and "up to no good." As author Megan McKenna and other female theologians have concluded, women didn't "count" in patriarchal cultures; moreover most women could not read. In the Roman Catholic tradition, Mary could be lifted up as a positive example. Out of bias—whether deliberate or as a cultural by-product, many strong feminine voices are ignored as examples of spiritual heroics and obedience. Miriam, Deborah, Jael, Huldah, and Esther were overlooked or only occasionally acknowledged. Storyteller Michael E. Williams underscores the impact of such a biblical tragedy:

The stories of women in the Bible have not traditionally received the attention they deserve. It is clear from the Hebrew narratives that God employed women's voices to speak God's word and women to enact God's will. It is also evident that many stories have women acting in both leadership and supporting roles whose presence makes an important difference in the way the story is told as well as its outcome. [27]

A couple of decades of women in theological seminaries and divinity schools as students and teachers and in local parishes as pastors, have challenged old prejudices. And the calling to rigorous theological research has resulted in the equipping of a cadre of women theologians who are giving us a fresh look at Bible stories. As a result, some males are smacking their foreheads and saying, "I never saw that before." Sadly, some of this research has been dismissed as "feminist" or agenda based. I have greatly profited by the gifts that Renita J. Weems, Phyllis Trible, Megan McKenna, and others are providing. As a believer who takes the Scripture seriously, I am being challenged by their work, and my faith is strengthened by their insight.

How would you identify yourself to a total stranger: I am male, single adult, self-employed, Caucasian, and so forth. Take a moment and fill in the blanks below:

I am _____.
I am _____.
I am _____.

These "I am" statements are the filters through which I read, hear, and use the Scripture; some of those can become barriers to the real message of liberation and grace. Simply because I am a single adult, and in particular, a divorced single adult, I am much more interested in what the Scripture really says about singleness.

Jesus used feminine imagery to convey his agony over Jerusalem: "O Jerusalem, Jerusalem—you murder the prophets, and you stone those sent to you! Oh, how often have I yearned to gather you together, like a hen gathering her chicks under her wings! But you would have none of it" (Matthew 23:37-38 *The Inclusive New Testament*). Jesus could have used some macho, tough guy analogy, but he didn't. If Jesus used the feminine voice, why can't I appreciate it?

"Let the point of a passage . . . come out naturally like the kernel of a hazel-nut; and not piecemeal, and after much trouble . . . like the kernel of a walnut." (Charles Simeon) [28]

By looking for and listening to the feminine voice in the Scripture, I have been challenged to see a feminine side of God, a tenderness that I prefer to the view of God I saw as a child—the judge with the long memory or the God I could not please. Through this reading, I have been reminded of the layered realities of the Scripture: reading the Bible can be like peeling the layers of an onion. Listening to the feminine voice begins with a question, "What have we here?"

The more I read from authors like Megan McKenna, and the more I listen to my single friends in ministry like Linda Quanstrom, Diane Swaim, Ilona Buzick, and Carolyne Teague, the more I wonder about the Scripture nudgings that invite me to explore and perhaps stretch some of my "I am" biases:

☐ *Jesus and the woman at the well.* A careful reading suggests that the first evangelist of the church was not Philip, but rather a five-times-divorced woman Jesus met at the well in Samaria. What could be more plain than, "Many Samaritans from that city believed in him *because of the woman's testimony"?* (John 4:39). We will have neighbors in heaven who are there because they first heard the "good news" from a woman with a marital resume that would make her a candidate for today's talk shows. Oddly, the people who always proof text Matthew 19:1-12 on divorce and remarriage, never seem to consider this account in John. I think the encounter is there, waiting for divorced people like me to trip over, so that we can sense that God is still the God of hope for the divorced.

☐ *Jesus and the woman caught in adultery.* I've heard lots of preaching on that passage but only recently has it dawned on me that it takes two to commit adultery: where was the man? And what was the woman's physical condition if "caught in adultery." Possibly naked?

☐ *Jesus and Lazarus, Mary and Martha.* What tone of voice did Mary use after her brother's death and Jesus' seemingly rude tardiness in responding to her panicked message, "Lord, he whom you love is ill" (John 11:3). Four days later after Lazarus had been buried, Jesus showed up concerned. Mary snapped, "Lord, if you had been here, my brother would not have died" (John 11:32). Is an exclamation mark missing here? What was her tone of voice? I think her words stung Jesus!

This passage illustrates how the Scripture can come to life when read with flair.

Practice repeating Mary's words using different tones of voice.

Although I have two earned doctorates in religion, there are two passages that I have never seen explained in commentaries or heard as the basis of sermons or writings, Luke 8:1-3 and Mark 15:41. Read this slowly, "Soon afterwards he went on through cities and villages, proclaiming and bringing the good news of the kingdom of God. The twelve were with him, *as well as some women* who had been cured of evil spirits and infirmities" (Luke 8:1-2). Women? In Jesus' entourage? Where was this verse when I was in Sunday school?

Before you boast, "I believe the whole Bible," you need to think through the implications. Many of us mean when we say this that we believe those passages we have chosen to believe without reservation. I have often asked, "If you believe the whole Bible, why don't you live as if you do?"

Women traveling with Jesus? From the stories and the pictures I learned, the disciples were all males. But the Scripture clearly says that women traveled with Jesus. And there's more. These women "provided for them out of their resources" (Luke 8:3*b*).

I almost want to scream, "What! Women as major donors?" In case I want to tiptoe around the implications, this text is supported by Mark's observation, "These [women] used to follow him and provided for him when he was in Galilee; and there were many other women who had come up with him to Jerusalem" (Mark 15:41). Women stayed at his dying and were the first to go to the tomb!

Recently, in a large single adult conference I witnessed the dismissal of the feminine voice. Two nationally known male single adult leaders were decrying males counseling women, suggesting that women lead to the "sexual fall" of men in ministry. "That's why I tell men," one leader exclaimed loudly, "*Never* counsel women!" Fortunately, for the audience, the moderator asked if either of the women on the panel wished to respond. My friend Carolyn Teague, a single adult with wide experience as a spiritual counselor of single adults, waited a moment then softly but poignantly said, "I am glad the Lord never operated under that philosophy of ministry. I am glad he had time for the woman at the well." A *whooosh!* went through the audience. One of the males snapped, "Jesus never counseled women!" I was so glad that Carolyn had lifted the feminine voice.

Identify a passage that raises the feminine voice.

_____

What does this particular passage say to you?

_____

For more information on women and the Scripture see:

McKenna, Megan, *Not Counting the Women and Children: Neglected Stories from the Bible* (Maryknoll, N.Y.: Orbis Books, 1994).

Trible, Phyllis, *Texts of Terror: Literary-Feminist Readings of Biblical Narratives* (Philaldelphia: Fortress, 1984).

Weems, Renita J., *Just a Sister Away: A Womanist Vision of Women's Relationships in the Bible* (San Diego: LuraMedia, 1988).

Williams, Michael E., ed., *The Storyteller's Companion to the Bible: Old Testament Women* (Nashville: Abingdon Press, 1993).

16. Reading Scripture Obediently ● ● ● ● ● ● ● ● ● ● ● ● ● ●

Why read the Bible if you are not going to obey?

"Be doers of the word, and not merely hearers who deceive themselves."—*James 1:22*

It is one thing to read the Scripture but quite another to apply it and then to obey it; or to read it ahead of the actual time of need. That's why the psalmist talked about "hiding the word" in his heart in order not to sin. While the Bible can be of great comfort, particularly in times of illness or distress, it can also be a source of great discomfort. I sometimes think, "I wish I hadn't read that!"

"Holy Spirit think through me till your ideas are my ideas." (Amy Carmichael) [29]

That's one reason I am a strong believer in the stories of the Bible, particularly the Old Testament stories of great courage. The story of Daniel in the lions' den is a powerful reminder of God's ability to care for me, even in situations when I may feel like a caged lion.

One passage that has haunted me is the story of a Persian queen named Vashti, married to an insensitive cad named Xerxes. After a seven-day orgy of drunkenness, the king desired to tease his guests with a "look what I have that you don't" technique. He summoned Vashti to parade her beauty (Jewish tradition says "in the nude") before this male assemblage. Vashti rightly refused to do so. An idiot aide named Memucan convinced Xerxes that Vashti had not only offended the king but also had established a precedent for disobedience of wives throughout the kingdom. Incredible social chaos would result unless Xerxes acted promptly and sternly.

Xerxes signed a decree proclaiming that every man should be ruler over his own household. And Xerxes agreed to give Vashti's position to someone else who was more obedient than she was. For years I read this passage, seeing Vashti's exit as mere background material, necessary in order to provide for the arrival of Esther who would save her people. My male filter got in the way of the story.

Now, I read that passage and see that there is a price for saying no. Vashti paid the full price. She could have stripped, pranced, and three weeks later still been the queen. At a cost, of course. I see her "no" and the subsequent consequences as a reality of many divorced persons, particularly women, in today's world. I often think of Vashti's courage when I want to say some financially or politically expedient "yes." I find the courage to say "no."

"Consecutive reading of biblical books forces everyone who wants to hear to put himself, or to allow himself to be found, where God has acted. . . . We become part of what once took place. . . . Forgetting and losing ourselves, we, too, pass through the Red Sea, through the desert, across the Jordan into the promised land. With Israel we fall into doubt and unbelief and through punishment and repentance experience again God's help and faithfulness. . . . We are torn out of our own existence and set down in the midst of the holy history of God on earth." (Dietrich Bonhoeffer) [30]

What is one passage of scripture in which you feel you have been "torn out" of your existence and "set down" in the midst of an incident that became "the holy history of God"?

_____.

Is there some passage of scripture you have tried to ignore, or to get away from its implications for your life? _____

What is the most difficult "no" you've had to say?

_____.

Dietrich Bonhoeffer left Nazi Germany in 1939 to take a teaching post at Union Theological Seminary in New York. He could have lived out the war years as a single adult in relative security. However, because of his reading of the Scripture and his understanding of obedience, he chose to go back to Germany to preach and teach. Finally, toward the end of the war, he was executed by the Nazis. Three key questions shaped the thinking and obedience of this brilliant theologian:

☐ What did Jesus mean to say to us?

☐ What is his will for us today?

☐ How can he help us to be good Christians in the modern world? [31]

Bonhoeffer's questions were sharpened on the anvil of his belief: "Jesus Christ is not dead, but alive and speaking to us today through the testimony of Scriptures. He comes to us today, and is present with us in bodily form and in his word. If we would hear his call to follow, we must listen where he is to be found, . . . Discipleship never consists in this or that specific action: it is always a decision, either for or against Jesus Christ." [32]

Bonhoeffer believed that the answers came from the careful but reflective study of the Scripture, the record of what God had done in the past, an indicator of what God would do in the future.

Bonhoeffer wrote so powerfully about what he called "cheap grace." "Cheap grace is the preaching of forgiveness without requiring repentance, baptism without church discipline, communion without confession, absolution without personal confession. Cheap grace is grace without discipleship, grace without the cross, grace without Jesus Christ, living and incarnate." [33] I would ask, without doing violence to Bonhoeffer, grace without the devotional life?

In *How to Give Away Your Faith*, Paul Little formulated questions that are helpful as we read the Scripture obediently.

Read through the questions before you read the Bible passage. Ask God to help you be open to these questions and to the prompting of the Holy Spirit as you read. You may want to select a smaller portion of the Scripture and give yourself time for a second reading before you tackle the questions. You may want to use your journal to record your encounter. In this particular passage of Scripture I will read ask: Is there an example for me to follow? Is there a sin for me to avoid? Is there a command for me to obey? Is there a promise for me to claim? What does the passage teach me about God or Jesus Christ? Is there a difficulty for me to explore? Is there something in this passage I should pray about today? [34]

It may be clearer to you now why it is easier to read informationally rather than formationally. It does not inconvenience or threaten us.

When two Southern sisters and slave owners read the Scripture, they had difficulty reconciling the practice of owning slaves. Not only did they free their own slaves, but they lobbied other Christians to do so. One of them, Angelina Grimke, daringly wrote a book, *Appeal to the Christian Women of the Southern States*, arguing that slavery was contrary to human law, the teachings of Jesus, and the Declaration of Independence. What Angelina wrote, sister Sarah declared from the podium. Needless to say this obeying the Scripture cost Sarah and Angelina their status in their wealthy Charleston society.

Angelina declared, "Don't say 'There is nothing I can do.' I know you do not make the laws, but I also know that you are the wives and mothers, the sisters and daughters of those who do; and if you really suppose you can do nothing to overthrow slavery, you are greatly mistaken. . . . 1st. You can read on this subject. 2nd. You can pray over this subject. 3rd. You can speak on this subject. 4th. You can act on this subject. . . . Try to persuade your husband, father, brothers and sons that slavery is a crime *against God and man.*"
(Angelina Grimke) [35]

Angelina's reading of the Scripture—in the Hebrew and Greek—convinced her that God never made a slave. Moreover, the Hebrews at least had provisions for the periodic freeing of slaves, while the Southern custom robbed the slave of his rights as a creature of God.

One hundred years later, a commitment to Scripture put Corrie ten Boom in conflict with the Nazis occupying Amsterdam during World War II. When she read the Scripture, she concluded the Jewish people were the "chosen children" of her God; therefore, she *had* to come to their aid. Corrie turned her home into a hiding place while many other Christians ignored the plight of Jewish people.

After reading the Scripture, Angelina courageously spoke out on a social issue of her day. Is there an issue in our culture you need to speak out on?

"Each one of us is an essential link in God's plan of saving the world." [36]

The truth behind the phrase in Anna Warner's song for children, "The Bible tells me so," has challenged many single adults to take stands, to invest their lives in great issues, and to make a difference. What will your reading lead to?

17. Reading Singularly •

I bring my singleness with me when I read the Scripture.

"All scripture is inspired by God and is useful for teaching, for reproof, for correction, and for training in righteousness." —*2 Timothy 3:16*

The first time a publisher approached me about writing on the single adults of the Bible, I responded that there were not enough single adults or sufficient details of their lives to do a book. Moreover, because of the Jewish commitment to having offspring "as numerous as the stars of the sky," there were few unmarried males. But I agreed to reflect on the issue. I made a list of the obvious single adults:
- ☐ Jesus
- ☐ Paul

- [ ] Jephthath's daughter who was sacrificed by her father
- [ ] Tamar who was raped by her half-brother, Amnon
- [ ] Diana who was sexually violated by a neighbor boy
- [ ] Mary, Martha, and Lazarus, friends of Jesus.

But the more I began to delve, the more my perception was stretched. It was as if they began to step out of the shadows of the Scripture.

God has always been concerned about single adults and has often invited single adults to be part of his great plans.

One day I suddenly realized that the eunuchs in the Scripture were single adults! Clearly God worked through eunuchs to accomplish divine purposes:

- [ ] Ebed-melech rescued Jeremiah from a pit where he would have died (Jeremiah 38:1-13; 39:15-18).
- [ ] The conversion of an unnamed Ethiopian eunuch set off a row in a family-values obsessed early church (Acts 8:26-40).

I also stumbled onto the courage of five single women who daringly challenged Moses' interpretation of family values and demanded the right to inherit property (Numbers 27:1-11). I can only imagine the astonishment (women did not inherit in that society) when God agreed with the single women, "The daughters of Zelophehad's are right in what they are saying; you shall indeed let them possess an inheritance. . . ."

The Scripture also identifies several widows:

- [ ] A widow whose mite attracted the attention of Jesus (Luke 21:1-2).
- [ ] A widow whose only son had died; Jesus halted the funeral procession and "gave him back" (Luke 7:11-15).
- [ ] The courageous widows Naomi and Ruth (Ruth 1–4).
- [ ] The widow whose two sons were being seized for the payment of her debts; in that day's financial reality, without pension, social security, welfare, she would have become destitute or a prostitute (2 Kings 4:1-7).

Consider James's staunch words, "Religion that is pure and undefiled before God, the Father, is this: to care for orphans and widows in their distress, and to keep oneself unstained by the world."—James 1:27

What does James 1:27 say to you?

Traditionally, the church has concerned itself with the last portion, "to keep oneself unstained by the world." Taking the first part of that verse seriously would challenge the financial realities of today's church that prefers to say, "Let insurance or the government take care of single parents," and then whines about welfare mothers. That's why we fast forward over verses that would financially inconvenience us, although still loudly proclaiming our belief in the inspiration of the "whole" Bible. But just try wrestling with the implications of this verse in Greek, since the word *chera* means not only "widow" but "one without a mate."

Jesus' caution about those who have eyes to see, but "fail to see" (Mark 8:18) is true of many single adult believers who do not take the Christian faith seriously. To read with a "first person singular" perspective means asking what the Scripture says about my reality as an unmarried adult. If more single adults were aware of how much the Bible has to say about single adults and to single adults, they would read it more.

18. Reading Interactively ●

When you read, *read!*

Robert Mulholland has noted our impatience with the Scripture: we want it to speak now; after all, we're people in a hurry. "There is also the need to be willing to wait upon the Word. There is the necessity of offering up our reading of the Scripture to God to be used *as* God chooses and *when* God uses."[38]

Reading the Scripture is something of an invitation: to wait, to ponder, to wonder, "What is God saying to me?" Megan McKenna is interested in how a passage makes the reader feel and poses these questions for the reader's consideration:

1. What does the Scripture make you feel?
2. Who is in the text? Where? When? What is happening?
3. Is there anything in the passage that makes you nervous, bothers, or upsets you?
4. What are you going to do as an individual to make this passage come true in your present life?[39]

These days there is great resurgence of interest in the stories of the Scripture. In *The Word Is Very Near You*, Martin L. Smith offers a comprehensive way to interact with a text. Take a moment to read the following story of a trio of travelers on the road to Emmaus, following the death of Jesus.

That same day two of them were walking to the village Emmaus, about seven miles out of Jerusalem. They were deep in conversation, going over all these things that had happened. In the middle of their talk and questions, Jesus came up and walked along with them. But they were not able to recognize who he was.

He asked, "What's this you're discussing so intently as you walk along?"

They just stood there, long-faced, like they had lost their best friend. Then one of them, his name was Cleopas, said, "Are you the only one in Jerusalem who hasn't heard what's happened during the last few days?"

He said, "What has happened?"

They said, "The things that happened to Jesus the Nazarene. He was a man of God, a prophet, dynamic in work and word, blessed by both God and all the people. Then our high priests and leaders betrayed him, got him sentenced to death, and crucified him. And we had our hopes up that he was the One, the One about to deliver Israel. And it is now the third day since it happened. But now some of our women have completely confused us. Early this morning they were at the tomb and couldn't find his body. They came back with the story that they had seen a vision of angels who said he was alive. Some of our friends went off to the tomb to check and found it empty just as the women said, but they didn't see Jesus."

Then he said to them, "So thick-headed! So slow-hearted! Why can't you simply believe all that the prophets said? Don't you see that these things had to happen, that the Messiah had to suffer and only then enter his glory?" Then he started at the beginning, with the Book of Moses, and went on through all the Prophets, pointing out everything in the Scriptures that referred to him.

They came to the edge of the village where they were headed. He acted as if he were going on but they pressed him: "Stay and have supper with us. It's nearly evening; the day is done." So he went in with them. And here is what happened: He sat down at the table with them. Taking the bread, he blessed and broke and gave it to them. At that moment, open-eyed, wide-eyed, they recognized him. And then he disappeared.

Back and forth they talked. "Didn't we feel on fire as he conversed with us on the road, as he opened up the Scriptures for us?" (Luke 24:13-35).[40]

Martin L. Smith suggests we approach Bible stories in this manner:

—Select a single story from the Bible. We will use Luke 24:13-35 to illustrate the technique.
—Spend some moments settling down before reading.
—Ask God to touch you through the passage of scripture you have chosen.
—Pick up your Bible and read the passage slowly and carefully several times. Pause between each reading. Notice the details. Ask questions.
—Put down the Bible. Give your imagination free rein to bring the scene to life as a participant. Hear. Smell. Taste. Look. Touch.
—Let the drama slowly unfold—there is no hurry.
—Talk to Jesus about what you are feeling. Tell him how this passage has touched you.
—Bring this time to a close with thanks to God and by saying the Lord's Prayer or a favorite psalm or by singing a chorus or a verse of a hymn.[41]

You can also read with your journal handy to jot down ideas, almost like a detective, but don't give in to the temptation to begin writing before you have mentally and soulfully interacted with the text.

In the story of the trio of travelers, consider these questions:

What was the time of day? _____

What was the season of the year? _____

What could you smell? _____

What sex were the two original travelers? _____

Describe their facial expression when they asked, "Are you the only one in Jerusalem who hasn't heard . . . ?" _____

Who else was on the road? _____

What was the condition of the road? _____

What was the facial description of the two when they recognized Jesus?

_____

What other questions came to your mind while reading?

_____

_____

Robert Mulholland rightly observed: When our reading of Scripture becomes dry and doesn't seem "to do" anything, for us anymore, our tendency is to look somewhere else. We look to the "Christian top ten" reading list, or the latest "bright light" in Christian literature . . . rather than to the Bible itself.[42]

Basil Pennington offers a second way to interact with the Scripture, a method he describes as "sacred reading."

—Approach the sacred text with reverence and call upon the Holy Spirit.

—For five minutes (or longer if you are so drawn), listen to the Lord speaking to you through the text and respond to him.

—At the end of the time, pick a word or phrase to take with you, and thank the Lord for being with you and speaking to you in this time together.

—Pray: "Holy Spirit, you who inspired the writer. You who live in us. Make the word come alive to us now."[43]

"WORDS fail to express my love for this holy book. My gratitude to its author, for his love and goodness: how shall I thank him for it?" (Lottie Moon)[44]

The best answer to Miss Moon's question may be by pausing and thanking God for granting us easy access to the Scripture. Pennington is quick to point out that this is not some surefire money-back system. "We listen for our allotted time. If the Lord speaks to us in the first word, we respond. If not, we just read on, listening, ready to respond."[45]

> "If we hope to make steady progress in our Christian life, probably nothing is more important than the discipline of having daily 'quiet times' with God. . . . Ideally, it is the first thing in the morning and last thing at night that we should keep a sacred engagement with God, although all of us have to decide what are the best times for us." (John Stott) [46]

Significantly, Stott calls for quiet times rather than a quiet time.

> "This morning, I ended the reading of my Bible through, in about four months. It is hard work to find time for this but all I read and write, I owe to early rising." (Francis Asbury) [48]

One has to wonder what Asbury would say about scheduling reading the Scripture in today's frantic pace!

Some days words or phrases leap off the page at us; other days, we select the word. In my experience, it may be hours later the word when I chose and the reality of my day intersect and all I say is a hushed, "Oh, my!" Time with the Word prepared me for the circumstance.

Pennington reminds, "I have found that this word that stands out proves to be just the word someone else needs from me as the day moves on."[47] The chosen word or phrase can "suddenly come alive" often when we least expect it.

19. Reading Other Sacred Writings ● ● ● ● ● ● ● ● ● ● ● ● ● ● ●

> "When you come, bring the cloak that I left with Carpus at Troas, also the books, and above all the parchments." —*2 Timothy 4:13*

God is still nudging authors with ideas the children of God need.

I have long found these words of Paul—a single adult—sobering. In his last days, he is asking for reading material. I understood his need when listening to my friend Joan, a pastor whose library burned in a church fire. You can replace the books, but not the way they were marked.

John Wesley, when a single adult, referred to himself as *homo unis libri*—a man of one book, the Bible, although he read very widely. One biographer needed fourteen pages to list the books Wesley had read as a young single. Among those were the Christian classics of Anglican, Lutheran, Roman, Orthodox, and Moravian traditions.

I came to understand the need for spiritual reading for texts that arouse or stimulate our longing for God as I immersed myself in reading Susan Howatch's *Glittering Images*—part of a seven novel series on the Church of England. Rarely do I underline in novels but Howatch's words "aroused" my "longing for God."

In the biographical reading I have done in order to write on single adults, I have been fascinated by their reading habits.

Lottie Moon, who helped shape the Southern Baptist commitment to missions, cherished a worn copy of Thomas á Kempis's *The Imitation of Christ*. In the margins she copied other devotional writings in French, German, Italian, and English. One particular day in 1902, physically exhausted, she read from Kempis, "There is nothing else that I am able to present more acceptable than to offer my heart wholly to God, and to unite it most inwardly to Him." Those words provided encouragement for that day's particular needs. [50]

Francis Asbury spent time reading and rereading William Law's *Serious Call* and Quaker pastor Richard Baxter's *Call to the Unconverted*. [51]

One of the greatest American pulpiteers was a single adult, Phillips Brooks, whose appetite for reading was as large as his physical girth. Since he traveled extensively, he carried books to read. He could tune out the distraction of the train and read works that touched his longing for God and found their way into his preaching. He had the habit of tossing finished books out the windows of trains, believing that someone would come along, find them, and read them.

Elisabeth Elliot, biographer of Amy Carmichael, founder of the Dohnavur Compound in India that rescued thousands of children from poverty and prostitution, commented about Carmichael's devotional reading. "She read like lightning," read widely, and was able to quickly separate the wheat in a book from the chaff. She was known to bring books to meals with her staff and to say, "Listen to this!" [52] Her reading included the great spiritual classics: *The Cloud of Unknowing, The Practice of the Presence of God* by Brother Lawrence, *Little Flowers of St. Francis*, William Penn's *No Cross, No Crown*, as well as books by Julian of Norwich, Evelyn Underhill, William Cowper, Saint Augustine, and many others. Old books were "wells" "from which she drew cold, pure refreshment." She dismissed much of contemporary writing as "sawdust." [53]

Here are some suggestions for "stretching" reading:

The Search for a Spiritual Life
- ☐ Sue Monk Kidd — *When the Heart Waits*
- ☐ Macrina Wiederkehr — *A Tree Full of Angels*

The Classics
- ☐ Augustine — *Confessions*
- ☐ Francis DeSales — *Introduction to the Devout Life*
- ☐ Madame Guyon — *Spiritual Letters*
- ☐ Dag Hammarskjöld — *Markings*
- ☐ Thomas á Kempis — *The Imitation of Christ*
- ☐ William Law — *A Serious Call to a Devout and Holy Life*
- ☐ Brother Lawrence — *Practicing the Presence of God*
- ☐ Evelyn Underhill — *The Spiritual Life*
- ☐ Thomas Kelly — *A Testament of Devotion*

Prayer
- ☐ John Baille — *A Diary of Private Prayer*
- ☐ *Anthony Bloom — *Beginning to Pray*
- ☐ — *The Book of Common Prayer*
- ☐ Richard Foster — *Prayer: Finding the Heart's True Home*
- ☐ *Richard Foster — *Prayers from the Heart*
- ☐ Emile Griffin — *Clinging Prayer*
- ☐ John Killinger — *Beginning Prayer*
- ☐ C. S. Lewis — *Letters to Malcolm on Prayer*
- ☐ Basil Pennington — *Called*
- ☐ Kenneth Swanson — *Uncommon Prayer: Approaching Intimacy with God*

Spiritual Disciplines
- ☐ Richard Foster — *Celebration of Discipline*
- ☐ Steve Harper — *Devotional Life in the Wesleyan Tradition*
- ☐ Morton T. Kelsey — *Adventure Inward*
- ☐ Robert Mulholland — *Shaped by the Word*
- ☐ *Susan Muto — *Pathways of Spiritual Living*
- ☐ Dallas Willard — *Spirit of the Disciplines*

Spiritual Pilgrimages
- ☐ Dietrich Bonhoeffer — *Life Together* / *Cost of Discipleship*
- ☐ *C. S. Lewis — *A Grief Observed* / *Mere Christianity*
- ☐ Brennan Manning — *The Lion and the Lamb*
- ☐ *Susan Muto — *Celebrating the Single Life*
- ☐ *Henri Nouwen — *In the Name of Jesus the Beloved* / *The Return of the Prodigal*

When Mary MacLeod Bethune was a child she was caught holding a book in a home where her mother was working as a maid. "Put down that book. You don't know how to read!" Mary was ordered by the homeowner's daughter.

"Well I'm going to learn," replied Mary.

The attitude of Mary MacLeod Bethune can become our attitude, too. "I am going to learn." Mary prayed, "Please, Lord Jesus, have someone teach me to read. . . ."[55]

It is easy to look at the length of the book list and to feel overwhelmed. Remember this is not a one-two-three "easy fix" program of reading. These books are "meat," works you will read and want to reread.

Read with some zest! Use your voice to make the Scripture come alive. If there is drama in the passage, make that drama come to life. These are not just words on a page as in a novel or a biography. This is sacred text given as a gift to today's single adult.

"Now, at last, I have the time to read. I realize that we tend to read the great books too early, before we have enough experience to understand them, and sometimes we never open then again. Such neglect is a serious mistake, which may be corrected." (Elton Trueblood) [56]

Where to Start?

☐ Ask God to guide you to the right books.

☐ Ask God to guide you to a reading companion familiar with the spiritual classics to guide you in your selection.

☐ Realize that these are not "soft," easy, "lite" spirituality books but are demanding. You may have to back up and reread a sentence or a paragraph. You may need to put aside the book for a while and come back to it.

☐ Read with a notebook or journal. In fact, this reading will provide you with "jump starts" for your journaling.

☐ Take the list to a pastor or spiritual friend and ask this person to recommend books for you. If you do not initially feel comfortable doing that, I would suggest starting with one on the list marked with an asterisk.

> "My variety of reading fare amuses me. . . I am a bookaholic. If there isn't a stack of unread books waiting on the corner of my desk, I grow jittery." (Eugenia Price) [57]

You may not find some of these books in the typical "Christian" bookstores, but they can order them for you. Also look in Roman Catholic bookstores or used book bookstores. Sadly, some friends may look with skepticism at the list because most of the writers are from either mainline Protestant faith traditions or are Catholics. Remember some of these books have stood the test of time. Some of these authors have paid dearly for their writings, even with their lives.

> "I realize now there would not have been any way I could have read the books I have read . . . if I had been encumbered by a husband and family." (Evelyn Ramsey) [58]

20. Reading to Memorize ●●●●●●●●●●●●●●●●●●●●

> Memorization is more an issue of spending time than of skill.

> "I treasure your word in my heart."—*Psalm 119:11*

In my undergraduate work, one professor had a most "discomfiting" prayer he used on exam days: "Bring to the students' minds that which they have studied: Bring to those who have not studied, repentance." I had to memorize the entire British monarchy for his history of England class. What would I ever need with that? Well, it was on the final exam. But that memorization has become a framework on which I hang historical events or even contemporary events in British history.

We don't always have a Bible handy and we can't always stop to look up a verse. But if we have memorized it, God will often bring it into our consciousness in a moment when we most need it.

Prisoners of war have reported remembering portions they learned as children. Widows have talked about verses that have come to comfort them in the night's loneliness. As a divorced person, I wrestled with a verse I had memorized as a child, "I will never leave you, or forsake you." Could I believe that?

> "If we diligently read the Bible, the Holy Spirit will give us the right words and scripture references. . . ." (Corrie ten Boom) [59]

I grew up in a tradition that deeply encouraged memorizing scripture. Sometimes people would stand in a service and recite their favorite verse of scripture. Every week children had a memory verse for Sunday school. In other church programs, we were encouraged to choose our own verse. I worked hard all week—after all, I wanted to get that gold star beside my name. Some of the verses I memorized were tongue twisters, so I wasn't happy when my friend David would quote the shortest verse in the Bible, "Jesus wept," which happened to be the favorite of the teacher, Mrs. Gwinn. Week after week he got the same gold star reward I received.

Now, many years later, I am still surprised when a verse "appears" out of my deep subconscious, in the moment I need it. Sometimes, the verse is not always word perfect, but its meaning comforts me. Even the author of the book of Hebrews did not always know "chapter and verse" and quoted Psalm 8:4-6, preceded with these words, "But someone has testified somewhere . . ." (Hebrews 2:6).

As a child, Corrie ten Boom had been encouraged by her father to memorize the Scripture in other languages. That paid off handsomely when she earned the nickname "God's tramp" for her evangelism around the world.

> "I am now memorizing certain verses of Scripture which I call my First Aid Course. These are emergency Scriptures which I apply to the wound until I can look up the rest of the Scriptures which will bring further healing."
> (Corrie ten Boom) [60]

Hints for Memorizing:

- [ ] Ask God to help you memorize.
- [ ] Take the verse a phrase at a time, building one phrase upon another.
- [ ] Type or write out the verse on a notecard and carry it with you, periodically referring to it. Post-it notes can be helpful. If you are washing dishes, put the note in front of you. It is part of the process of "redeeming the time." Brother Lawrence used his pots-and-pans washing time to pray.
- [ ] Before you memorize, read the verse over and over, letting it sink into your mind.
- [ ] Imagine the verse. Are there key words that can become the skeleton on which most of the verse hangs?
- [ ] If you have children, memorize verses with them.
- [ ] I find it helpful to repeat the verse as I go to sleep.

One great aid to memorizing is to read the Bible aloud. In centuries past, particularly before the invention of printing, most people heard rather than read the Scripture.

> "Blessed is the one who reads aloud the words of the prophecy, and blessed are those who hear and who keep what is written in it."
> —Revelation 1:3

You can read aloud in a worship or small group setting, with a friend, or by yourself. Imagine that you are hearing the words for the first time. Reading in a new translation will give added impact to the words.

Read some of your favorite passages into a tape recorder. Then you can take the tape with you for commuter traffic snarls or on long drives.

> "Gratitude exclaims, very properly, "How good of God to give me this." (C. S. Lewis) [61]

> *Read* it to be wise.
> *Believe* it to be safe.
> *Practice* it to be holy." (Henrietta Mears) [62]

Remember you are memorizing not like an army storing up ammunition for a future battle, but as a resource for you, and occasionally, for others. Sadly, too many single adults have memorized a passage and later used it as a bludgeon to wound someone. Scripture can bruise the soul, and never discolor the skin. I was saddened by a newspaper clipping about a man sentenced to two years probation for hitting and choking a woman he was dating. The fight started when she disagreed with his interpretation of a scripture verse.

I became sensitive to this misuse of memorized scripture during my divorce. An incredible number of well-intentioned people felt "led" to "share" Romans 8:28 (which they had memorized for such an encounter) and then hit the "play" button: "All things work together for good"—the same way a disc jockey cues up a tape to reduce lag time. What I needed was someone to listen to me. Too often, all the quoter could or would offer was only a verse of scripture.

We also memorize so we do not forget that God has had a long tradition of using flawed people whose biographies were often soiled. So, when my biography became soiled, I began to appreciate more the fact that:

- Moses stuttered.
- John Mark got "laid off" by the apostle Paul.
- David got his neighbor pregnant (and then killed her husband).
- Abraham and his son Isaac both lied to the same king about their relationships with their wives, claiming they were only "sisters."
- Elijah experienced burnout fatigue.
- A middle-age single named Ezekiel couldn't handle teasing about his bald head.
- Noah got drunk as a skunk.
- Lot's daughters got him drunk in order to sleep with him.
- John "streaked" to get away from the scene of the Crucifixion.
- Peter, James, and John napped while Jesus prayed alone in the garden.
- Tamar disguised herself as a roadside prostitute to snare her father-in-law.
- Peter was a loud mouth.
- Jacob was a mama's boy and a liar.
- Jonah was a bigot.

But somehow, our great God changed them and used them. We not only memorize the exact words and verses but also the stories of this long succession of very ordinary people—some of whom were unmarried—who God, in time, turned into *extra*ordinary people.

Section 3

21. Praying the Landscape of Our Minds • • • • • • • • • •

"Now I lay me down to sleep" won't cut it in this stress-centered world.

"Pray in the Spirit at all times in every prayer and supplication." —*Ephesians 6:18*

You have heard the spiritual, "Not my brother, not my sister, but it's me, O Lord, standing in the need of prayer." I find the honesty of the confession refreshing: "It's me," which is repeated six times in the chorus. Many single adults have found themselves praying/pleading, "It's *me*, O Lord, standing in the need of prayer." I once saw a cartoon of a man praying. A voice in the heavens demanded, "Will He know what this is regarding?" Oh yes, he will. Paul encourages us—no doubt from first-hand experience as a single adult, to pray with all kinds of prayers and requests. All kinds?

"What a man is on his knees before God, that he is—and nothing more." (Robert M. McCheyne) [1]

"Never doubt that the Lord hears our prayers even the unusual ones!" (Corrie ten Boom) [2]

What is the most unusual prayer that you have prayed?

_____

Did you pray it publicly or privately?

_____

How did you feel about that prayer at the time?

_____

What happened?

_____

How do you feel remembering that prayer now?

_____

Some of us overly rely on "Hail Mary!" prayers—even if we are not Roman Catholic—when we need a miracle, now! "Borderline" prayers are those exclamations, such as when we slap our forehead and groan, "O dear God!" Seeing a car crossing the center stripe and heading straight toward us converts us into pray-ers; or when we receive distressing news, "O God, no!" That's prayer, too.

> "Praying is not an experience reserved for a holy elite, but a mode of physical, functional, and spiritual survival. The choice is ours: we can erect barriers between ourselves and God, close doors, mete out love in stingy dribbles, and reap the meager results; or we can love God with our whole heart, soul, mind, and strength, pray without ceasing, and become the fully alive [single adult] he wants us to be."
> (Susan Muto) [3]

> "We say we believe God to be omniscient; yet a great deal of prayer seems to consist of giving Him information." (C. S. Lewis) [4]

> Prayer is surfing the landscape of the mind. Whatever is on our mind is a valid subject for prayer.

Some single adults don't want to demand too much of God, or interrupt God, believing that God is preoccupied with global crises and such. So they dash in, blurt out what they need, and move on. Others have become so proficient at manipulative/persuasive techniques that they try to guilt God, "God you know I need my child support money by 10 A.M. on Wednesday." "You know the singles' conference needs your help."

One of the great old gospel songs of the church is "What a Friend We Have in Jesus." Perhaps you remember a grandparent singing it. Unfortunately, some people think it is too sentimental for contemporary Christians to sing. But, every so often in my devotional time, I dig out an old hymnal, sit down at the keyboard, and play this and other songs I remember my grandfather Eckert singing:

> What a Friend we have in Jesus, All our sins and griefs to bear!
> What a privilege to carry Everything to God in prayer!
> O what peace we often forfeit,
> O what needless pain we bear,
> All because we do not carry Everything to God in prayer. [5]

Take a moment and ask God to quiet your mind. Now, reread the words of the gospel song. Pause. Breathe deeply. Slowly reread the lyrics. What word or phrase leaps out at you? Take a moment to reflect on what it is saying to you, what you want to say back. Breathe deeply. Now resume reading, giving another word or phrase an opportunity to interact with you. Breathe deeply again. Go back and reread the lyrics from the beginning. What word or phrase leaped out at you?

_____

What came to your mind as you reflected on that word or phrase?

_____

Take a moment to thank the Lord for this encounter.

_____

The word that leaped out at me was *"everything."* Or "every thing." "And honey, I do mean every thing!" as one friend reminds me. "Well," you counter, "I wouldn't want to bother God with such a teensy little request." Why not? Teensy little requests have a way of becoming big problems because we did not "carry everything to God in prayer."

Did you notice that Joseph Scriven, the author, mentioned *everything* twice. That encouraged me in moments when I am tempted to self-edit my prayer or to not bring up certain topics or issues, especially ones related to my sexual drives and struggles or my spending habits. "Everything" includes every thing.

> Whatever we consider "everything" in prayer will not surprise or shock God.

Maybe this is your "everything" moment. After reading and reflecting on this passage, perhaps you now have courage to verbalize the prayer you "need" to carry to God. This could be the moment for you to be courageous enough to bring "everything" to God in prayer.

> God, why is it that I am shy only about certain topics with you? Give me the courage to pray as openly about _____ as I talk about it to my friends or as frequently as I think about it. Amen.

> "People often ask me if the Lord actually speaks to me. All I know is that I keep answering back." (Henrietta Mears) [6]

22. Praying the Lord's Prayer ● ● ● ● ● ● ● ● ● ● ● ● ● ● ●

> The Lord's Prayer functions like a software on a computer, it is there to help you.
>
> "This is how you should pray . . ."—*Matthew 6:9 NIV*

One way to make single adults really anxious is to ask about their prayer habits. Two tough words are found in this verse: *should* (the favorite word of some Christians) and *pray*. I think it can be read "This is how you *can* pray." God does not want to *should* us into praying. Instead, God wants us to know that we have access when we cannot formulate our own prayers. Indeed, this is probably the most frequently prayed prayer in the world.

Jesus—a single adult—gave us an incredible gift when he instructed his disciples to pray: "Our Father in heaven, hallowed be your name. Your kingdom come. Your will be done, on earth as it is in heaven. Give us this day our daily bread. And forgive us our debts, as we also have forgiven our debtors. And do not bring us to the time of trial, but rescue us from the evil one." —Matthew 6:9-13

Fifty-seven words, four commas, and six periods. That's it. Simple and paradoxically so complex. You could memorize it in less than half an hour; yet, even after a lifetime, there is still mystery in this prayer. Understanding this simple, but complex prayer is like peeling the layers of an onion. Amazingly, thousands of single adults are relearning this prayer through Twelve Step programs when they, after baring their souls, reach out and take a hand and begin, "Our Father." Hundreds of books have been written on this misnamed "Lord's Prayer." More accurately it should be called the "Disciples' Prayer" or Our Prayer. John Friel had it right when he observed: "When Christ gave his followers the Lord's Prayer . . . he was saying, 'Keep it simple.'"[7]

This prayer hints that Jesus knew there would be times we would have trouble composing a prayer—whether in anger, desperation, fatigue, illness, or fear. So, Jesus offered a ready-made prayer, a prayer for all occasions. One prayer that instantly is rememberable. Sure, most of us still stumble over debts/trespasses. I have learned a way to circumvent that confusion by using the word *sin*. "Forgive us our *sins*, as we forgive those who have *sinned* against us." That choice helps me avoid little linguistic games. It's far more realistic.

I think this prayer is particularly helpful for the divorced. It's hard to pray the Lord's Prayer and have a laundry list of your ex's— and the other party's—faults, trespasses, and debts. Oh, it is tempting to remind the Lord of a few specifics—a reality that in other settings would be labeled tattling. But how do you know your ex-spouse is not mentioning your sins and shortcomings to God?

You may be wondering about the absence of "For yours is the kingdom, and the power, and the glory forever." That was not in the earliest manuscripts, and does not appear in many translations. I would rather read, "For *mine* is the kingdom, and the power, and the glory forever." Generally, we pray out of our thinking and we generally think in the first person singular mode: me, me, me. Personally, I am glad that Jesus used the first person plural pronoun, *Our* father rather than my father.

I constantly trip over the words, "Your will be done," because much of my praying is trying to convince God to do what I want to be done and when I want it done. I want God to rubber stamp my will and to "go along" with my goals, schemes, and ambitions.

I can pray the Lord's Prayer confidently because of the sentence Jesus used to introduce the prayer, "For your Father knows what you need before you ask him" (Matthew 6:8). Well, some single adults retort, "Then He knows that I need to be married to be a whole person! So why hasn't God answered that prayer, huh?"

"And shall I pray Thee change Thy will My Father, Until it be according to mine? But no, Lord, that never shall be, rather I pray Thee blend my human will unto thine." (Amy Carmichael) [8]

"Hallowed be Thy name, *not mine*, Thy kingdom come, *not mine*, Thy will be done, *not mine*, Give us peace with Thee Peace with men—Peace with ourselves, And free us from all fear." (Dag Hammarskjöld) [9]

"Insistence on certain things, on certain results, or specific requests can result in disaster. But asking for guidance has never failed." (Stella Dysart) [10]

What emotions are stirred when you read, "For your Father knows what you need before you ask him"? Circle or highlight words in Matthew 6:8 that trouble you. Now respond to those words: Well, if this verse is true, how come?

_____

_____

How would you share that verse with an angry single adult who snarls, "Well, if God knows my needs, how come he hasn't given me a spouse?" First of all, I would

_____

_____.

Or, I would ask them to think about the possibility that

_____

_____.

How does this version "touch" you?

_____

I am
- [ ] comfortable
- [ ] uncomfortable with this version. Why?

_____

Now, read it silently. Pause a moment to highlight any word or phrase that touches you. Now pray this version aloud, each time emphasizing different words.

You may want to be adventuresome. Listen to this rendition: "Abba God, hallowed be your name! May your reign come. Give us today tomorrow's bread. Forgive us our sins, for we too forgive everyone who sins against us; and don't let us be subjected to the Test." [12]

Father, help me to come to you with all those well-rehearsed questions that trouble me. That anger me. Father, give me the patience to wait on your answers, rather than supplying my own. Amen.

By this point in our lives, single adults have prayed the Lord's Prayer by rote so many times, that we seldom ponder what we are praying. Reading it (Matthew 6 and Luke 11) in another version can be helpful:

> Father, Reveal who you are.
> Set the world right.
> Keep us alive with three square meals.
> Keep us forgiven with you and forgiving others.
> Keep us safe from ourselves and the Devil. [11]

Perhaps, you would like to unleash your creativity on this prayer. Put this prayer into your own words. Remember this is a first draft; you can come back to this exercise throughout your reading.

_____

_____

_____

23. Praying the Jesus Prayer ● ● ● ● ● ● ● ● ● ● ● ● ● ● ● ●

It's easy to intimidate or harangue yourself for not praying. Yet, if even Jesus' disciples had to ask for tutoring, why shouldn't today's disciples need instruction? Before giving them the "Lord's Prayer," Jesus offered his disciples some simple guidelines on prayer.

☐ "Whenever you pray, go into your room and shut the door and pray to your Father who is in secret" (Matthew 6:6). Jesus subtly implies that we should be unseen as well. Earlier he had cautioned, "Beware of practicing your piety before others in order to be seen [or heard or praised] by them" (Matthew 6:1).

☐ "When you are praying, do not heap up empty phrases as the Gentiles do; for they think that they will be heard because of their many words" (Matthew 6:7). You don't have to "wear down" Jesus by whining.

☐ Jesus linked praying and forgiving, by declaring, "But if you do not forgive others, neither will your Father forgive your trespasses" (Matthew 6:15). If we pray, "It's her, it's her, O Lord," under the Spirit's direction we may soon hear ourselves praying, "It's me, it's me, O Lord."

One of the oldest prayers known to believers is the Jesus Prayer. This prayer exists in a couple of variations: "Lord Jesus Christ, have mercy on me." Seven simple words. Or, "Lord Jesus Christ, Son of the living God, have mercy on me."

"Oh, how we need the quiet times to let God speak to us." (Belle Bennett) [13]

These words are based on the prayer of blind Bartimaeus, who passionately cried out as Jesus passed nearby, "Jesus, Son of David, have mercy on me!" (Mark 10:47). The Jesus Prayer is simply verbalizing this classic prayer, inhaling on "Lord Jesus Christ," exhaling on "have mercy on me." The prayer is prayed by Ph.D's as well as drugstore clerks. Its simplicity reminds us that prayer does not have to be complicated to get God's attention or to be effective. And what do you need more than Jesus' mercy?

In the spaces below write in what you routinely ask for in your prayers.

_____   _____   _____
_____   _____   _____
_____   _____   _____

When was the last time you specifically asked for mercy?

_____

Basil Pennington suggests praying the Jesus Prayer twenty minutes in the morning and twenty minutes in the evening. Twenty minutes times two—why, that's forty minutes! "But I'm a busy single adult. I don't have time to spend forty minutes praying!" All right, start with two minutes praying the Jesus Prayer in the morning and two minutes in the evening; then slowly increase the time.

Spiritual fitness is like physical fitness: If fitness is a desired result, you have to budget time to "do" the things that lead to fitness. How much time do you spend:

watching TV	_____	personal hygiene	_____
working out	_____	working	_____
eating	_____	at church	_____
sleeping	_____	praying	_____

To the single adult who would respond, "But I'm too busy to pray!" how would you respond? _____

Take a moment and reflect on the slogan on the T-shirt. Assuming the left T-shirt is the front side, what message would you write on the back of the T-shirt? Now write it on the T-shirt below.

Many mornings when I am home, I sit in my rocker or in a stuffed chair in the den and pray the Jesus Prayer. One morning I found myself singing the prayer. I had composed a little tune, which I repeat four times. I find the Jesus Prayer calming. I am not asking Jesus for anything other than mercy for me and for others. And I can use this prayer as a framework or launch point for my other prayers.

Sometimes, I begin with a time of quiet, letting my body catch up with my soul. Then I pray the Jesus Prayer. In the third segment, I mention issues that I will be facing or have faced that day. I mention people who need Jesus' touch. I thank the Lord for the time. Then I resume the Jesus Prayer. "Lord, have mercy on _____." Sometimes in those quiet moments, the Lord has shown me how I can show mercy toward that individual. The Lord often needs to remind us that we can answer some of our own prayers. He regularly invites us to cooperate with the answers.

"O Lord, bless Sally. You know she is a single parent with those three kids. You know her ex-husband is driving a new Mercedes and is way behind in alimony and child support! Lord, bless Sally!"

"Why don't *you* 'bless' Sally?"

Our tendency is to turn up the volume, "O LORD, BLESS SALLY!!!" Often the Lord will use us—if we are willing—to be the vehicles or delivery system for his answer to prayer.

We make prayer so complicated. It's as simple as, "Lord Jesus Christ, have mercy on me."

"None of us is so rushed that it would be impossible to allow for even ten minutes in the day, in the morning or the evening, in which arrangements could be made for silence, allow it to speak, question it, and thereby look deep within and far beyond oneself. One might have a few verses of the Bible to read, but it is best to freely allow the soul to take its own way to the Father's house, to the homeland in which it finds peace." (Dietrich Bonhoeffer) [14]

Take two minutes and pray the Jesus Prayer. First, ask Jesus to help you pray this classic prayer: "Lord Jesus Christ, have mercy on me." Now, jot down a few of your initial impressions.

I felt _____.
I wondered about _____.
I found my mind _____.
Write the date of these impressions: _____.
At some point you will want to come back and reread these initial responses to praying the Jesus Prayer.

"If I could hear Christ praying for me in the next room, I would not fear a million enemies. Yet distance makes no difference. He *is* praying for me." (Robert McCheyne) [15]

It's hard to improve on silence.

"Be still before the LORD, and wait patiently for him." —*Psalm 37:7*

"In a noise-polluted world it is even difficult to hear ourselves think, let alone try to be still and know God. Yet it seems essential for our spiritual life to seek some silence, no matter how busy we may be. Silence is not to be shunned as empty space, but to be befriended as fertile ground for intimacy with God." (Susan Muto) [16]

"We are so afraid of silence that we chase ourselves from one event to the next in order not to have to spend a moment alone with ourselves, in order not to have to look at ourselves in the mirror." (Dietrich Bonhoeffer) [17]

"Father in heaven! Thou dost speak to man in many ways; . . . Even when thou art silent, still thou speakest to him. . . . Oh, in the time of silence when man remains alone, abandoned when he does not hear thy voice, it seems to him doubtless that the separation must last forever. Oh, in the time of silence when a man consumes himself in the desert in which he does not hear thy voice, it seems to him doubtless that it is completely extinguished. Father in heaven! It is only a moment of silence in an intimacy of conversation. Bless then this silence as thy word to man; grant that he never forgets that thou speakest also when thou art silent; . . . in thy silence as in thy word thou art still the same Father. . . ." (Søren Kierkegaard) [19]

It's one of the great clichés in our society, "Don't just sit there—say something!" Sometimes, the soul is benefited by the reverse, "Don't just say something—sit there." One August evening driving along the Carolina coast with a friend, we realized an incredible sunset was in the making. I pulled off the road and we walked to a grassy knoll and sat in silence simply watching the sun go down in a spirited splash of color. Neither of us had vocabulary to capture what we had just experienced; but the sunset was enhanced for us by the shared experience and by the silence. "Thanks, God, I needed that!"

Sometimes good friends or lovers simply sit in silence. Arnold Lobel won the hearts of children (and adults) with his writing about the friendship of Toad and Frog. One of his stories, "Alone" can be related to the prayer of silence.

Frog and Toad stayed on the island all afternoon. They ate wet sandwiches without iced tea. They were two close friends sitting alone together.[18]

Sometimes words are unnecessary; one simply basks in "being with" the friend, the loved one. All of us have known the comfort of just being held. So it is with prayer. Sometimes you simply need to sit in silence with the Lord; in the words of scripture, to be "still before the LORD." The next time you start to reach for the noise of the television or radio, reach for silence instead.

I have difficulty with the silence of God. Sometimes I fear I keep verbalizing my prayers so that I won't risk hearing God say something back—something I would rather not hear. I laughed at a cartoon of a man kneeling, looking toward heaven and saying, "Lord, if my prayers are pleasing to Thee, please confirm by fax." Sometimes, God confirms in the silence.

Let's put silence into practice. Get comfortable with your posture. Turn off any radio, TV, or CD. Take a couple of good breaths. Close your eyes and repeat Søren Kierkegaard's prayer, "O Lord, bless this silence."

What did you experience?_____

"God always answers us in the deeps, never in the shallows of our soul." (Amy Carmichael) [20]

"To preserve the silence within—amid all the noise. To remain open and quiet, a moist humus in the fertile darkness when the rain falls and the grain ripens—no matter how many tramp across the parade ground in whirling dust under an arid sky." (Dag Hammarskjöld) [21]

"Many people rely on their cars to provide a place of silence. I know I do. The time spent driving to and from the office is time I set aside for silence: no radio, some attempt to still rambling thoughts, focusing only on the hum of tires along the road." (Susan Muto) [22]

We are people addicted to racket and background noise. The radio offers plenty of both. So the next time you start your car and automatically reach for the radio, pull your hand back and say, "I think I will opt for a little silence today." And don't tell me that your car won't run without the radio going.

Single parents may need to adapt a disciplinary device for themselves, the old "Go to your room!" Some have set aside a room or a space; a single adult friend wrote her doctoral dissertation in a closet. Maybe you have a closet, a corner, a space for quiet sitting. Even your children could get involved in practicing silence.

Indeed, some of us walk in the door and encounter an auditory avalanche: stereos, TVs, phones, children, roommates. How differently our days would end if we could claim the privilege of fifteen minutes or more of silence! You can begin in your car. Just because you have a radio doesn't mean you have to use it all the time.

25. Praying the A-C-T-S ● ● ● ● ● ● ● ● ● ● ● ● ● ● ● ●

If Jesus' disciples had to ask, "Lord, teach us to pray," why should we be too intimidated to ask for the same instruction?

"Lord, teach us to pray . . ."—*Luke 11:1*

"Lord, teach me to pray."

I am amazed by the number of people who feel intimidated by their prayer life. They think they should have mastered prayer. Many hate praying in public or pray in King James-like phrases and use a tone of voice a friend calls "stained-glass voice."

One of the most effective prayer "techniques" to practice praying is A-C-T-S. The prayer is simply divided into four components: adoration, confession, thanksgiving, and supplication.

Adoration is praising God for who he is. Most of us tend to thank God for what he has done, is doing, and will do. Adoration thanks God for his character.

Confession is being honest with God; telling him what he already knows. Some single adults are anxious to "remind" God that since our ex-spouse is too busy to confess, we will do it for him/her. By the time we get around to our confession, the timer is running. "OOPS, gotta run."

Thanksgiving is expressing gratitude to God for his outrageous goodness to us—even when our lifestyle is a little on the economic lean. Thanksgiving is more for our benefit than for God's. Certainly it is not "paving the way" for the latest requests or "trying to get on God's good side." Rather, as we remember what God has done for us in the past, we gain the confidence to ask for current needs and to trust his provision for our future needs—not to be confused with our wants.

Supplication is bringing to God those issues on our minds and hearts. Some traditions talk about "coming boldly before the throne of grace"—praying gutsy; praying intentionally; praying with the it-never-hurts-to-ask perspective; taking Jesus at his word, "Ask, and it will be given you; search, and you will find" (Matthew 7:7).

The purpose of supplication is not to get gifts. Rather, it is to get to know the Giver who gives the gifts. Sadly, some of our relationships with God are dysfunctional on our part. God has every right to say, "I hear from you only when you want something." Have you ever snarled, "I wonder what she wants this time?" when a certain friend or acquaintance calls? That's why the A-C-T-S formula is such a great way to pray. The A-C-T-S keeps the asking in balance.

Billy Graham's niece wrote of overhearing Corrie ten Boom pray. "I seemed to hear the Lord say, 'Ah, Corrie, what can I do for you today?' She constantly expected."[23]

Put down the book and take a moment to clear your mind. Review what you've read on A-C-T-S. In the space below, compose a prayer using this formula.

A: _____

_____

C: _____

_____

T: _____

S: _____

_____

Which element of the four was the most difficult for you? Why?

_____

_____

Lord, this is terribly embarrassing.
I am supposed to know how to pray.
Effectively. Efficiently. Productively.
Everyone assumes that I know how to pray.
Everyone assumes that I pray.
I don't want anyone to know what you
    know—that I don't pray.
I am supposed to be able to pray to get results,
    to get your attention.
I am supposed to—but I don't have a clue.
But I do want to learn to talk to you, with you.
Can you help me pray?
If I come and spend time with you will you
    come?
Teach me to pray.

26. The Prayer of Adoration ●●●●●●●●●●●●●●●●●●

"Adoration is the lifting up of the heart and mind to God, asking nothing but to enjoy God's presence."—*Book of Common Prayer*

"Give thanks to the LORD, for his steadfast love endures forever."—*2 Chronicles 20:21*

Adoration turns our attention to the greatness of God. This is a time to concentrate on the outrageously extravagant grace of God. We are all tempted to turn prayer into a recounting of God's goodness based on what we have received. We are like children initially sorting through our Halloween candy: "Oh, I got this. I like this!"

The goal of adoration is to focus on the nature and person of God. One of the Old Testament stories that demonstrates adoration and reminds me to pray adoringly is 2 Chronicles 20. As the Israelites prepared to square off against their fierce warrior enemies, the Moabites and Ammonites, the predicted outcome was not good. Jahaziel urged the people, "Do not fear or be dismayed at this great multitude; for the battle is not yours, but God's" (20:15). You can almost hear the murmured, "That's easy for you to say!"

Look up 2 Chronicles 20:14-30. What is their prayer? (Hint: see verse 21.) The Israelites are instructed "Give thanks to the Lord." Why?

_____

_____

Have you ever faced a circumstance where you declared, "The battle is not mine, but the Lord's"? When?

How would you paraphrase this verse in light of some "vast" problem you are facing? "Do not be afraid for

_____

_____."

At a crucial moment, King Jehoshaphat appointed individuals "to sing to the LORD" and "praise him in holy splendor" (v. 21). On the eve of battle, they praised the Lord not for what he had done or for what they hoped he would do (save them from annihilation), but rather, for who he is: the splendor of his holiness. This is adoration. The next day, the singers placed themselves before the front line of the army and sang, "Give thanks to the LORD, for his steadfast love endures forever" (v. 21).

The Scripture reports that victory over their enemies came not as they began to fight but "as they began *to sing and praise*, the LORD set an ambush against the Ammonites, . . ." and they were defeated. In fact, the two armies destroyed each other rather than their mutual enemy: the Israelites. Imagine General H. Norman Schwarzkopf placing a great choir in front of his troops and ordering "Sing!" when the American army moved toward the sands of Iraq during Desert Storm!

Real love does not say, "I love you for all the good things you do for me." Rather, real love says, "I love you for who you *are!*" God wants to be loved for his character, not just for his ability to deliver the goodies and trinkets.

27. The Prayer of Confession ● ● ● ● ● ● ● ● ● ● ● ● ● ● ●

"Confession is good for the soul" is not just a cliché, but a spiritual and psychological reality.

"Create in me a clean heart, O God, and put a new and right spirit within me." —*Psalm 51:10*

Why is confession "good for the soul"?

_____

_____

What is the hardest thing you have ever confessed?

_____

_____

I have so appreciated the Anglican prayer of confession:

Almighty God, to you all hearts are open, all desires known, and from you no secrets are hid: Cleanse the thoughts of our hearts by the inspiration of thy Holy Spirit, that we may perfectly love thee, and worthily magnify thy holy Name; through Christ our Lord. Amen.[24]

This prayer could accurately be nicknamed, the "gotcha!" prayer. It complements the great prayer of David found in Psalm 51, which begins, "Create in me a clean heart, O God."

Take a moment and pray David's confession. Pause a moment. Now pray the prayer, emphasizing a different key word each time.

Create in me a pure heart, O God.

Create *in me* a pure heart, O God, and so forth.

After doing this, I feel:

_____

_____

However, even David hedged his guilt by praying, "Against you, you only, have I sinned and done what is evil in your sight." In fact, David had sinned against Bathsheba, Uriah (her husband), his own wives, his children, *and* had sinned against those who loved their king and looked up to him as a moral role model.

Sometimes, it is tempting to try a speedy confession, as if we are plea bargaining for a reduced punishment. Confession means meditating on our failures and sins until we have a better understanding of the real issues. We are often tempted to focus on what happened and never get around to why it happened.

A book title caught my attention recently, *Yes, Lord, I Have Sinned, But I Have Several Excellent Excuses* (James W. Moore, Abingdon Press). That title captures the mood of many single adults. For years, comedian Flip Wilson perfected his routine of a outrageously naughty single adult named Geraldine who always qualified her sin with, "The devil made me do it!" The devil could not be up to half the stuff he gets blamed for!

Confession involves accepting responsibility for our sins. This has been an issue in many divorces and in most romantic breakups: "It's *all* his/her fault." Indeed, American divorce law for years were based on the foe/adversary relationship. "Whose fault is it?" called one the "innocent party" and the other, the "guilty party." Both parties showed up in court "armed for bear." No issue was too minor to use.

Many abusers blame their victims rather than accept responsibility: "She made me so angry . . . he taunted me . . . I only did X because she did Y!" It's difficult to honestly admit, "I became so angry at you!" rather than "You made me so angry!"

Many single adults do better confessing the sins of commission, "I did this . . ." than the equally destructive sins of omission, "I failed to . . ."

Confession involves confronting both what we have done and what we have failed to do. Confessing our fear of risking is a tremendous step. Sometimes we cannot imagine doing what needs to be done, at least, in our own strength.

"O God, since You have enabled me to do the simple things that I could do, I have full trust in You to do the great things which I cannot do." (Lillian Thrasher) [25]

Isaac Watts, the great British hymn writer penned strong words on confession: "We ought to confess our more particular sins, which the world knows not, and pour out our whole souls before God, with great freedom and plainness: tell him all our follies, our infirmities, our joys, and sorrows: our brightest hopes, and our most gloomy and dismal fears, and all the inward workings of our hearts, either towards himself, or towards the creatures." [26]

Watts added that prayer is "correspondence" with "our kind and condescending friend." [27]

Most merciful God, we confess that we have sinned against thee in thought, word, and deed, by what we have done, and by what we have left undone. We have not loved thee with our whole heart; we have not loved our neighbors as ourselves. We are truly sorry and we humbly repent. For the sake of thy Son Jesus Christ, have mercy on us and forgive us; that we may delight in thy will, and walk in thy ways, to the glory of thy Name. Amen.[28]

Can you remember the last time you poured out "your whole soul" to God? If it's past time for a good soul-stirring confession, why not schedule one? You can start with the Anglican prayer of confession on page 72, note 24. Use the words of the confession as a starter and see what happens. Confession is taking a load off our souls.

Because some of us have difficulty composing a "good" full confession, some single adults have found this "penitential" confession a starting point.

Step 1: Read through the prayer silently.

Step 2: Read the prayer aloud, one sentence at a time, pausing to let the words resonate. You may wish to add specifics or to ask God to show you some.

Step 3: At the end of the written prayer, pause. Are there items you wish to add?

Step 4: Read aloud, "If we say that we have no sin, we deceive ourselves, and the truth is not in us. If we confess our sins, he who is faithful and just will forgive us our sins and cleanse us from all unrighteousness" (1 John 1:8-9).

Step 5: Say: "God, I dare to accept this promise. Amen."

In the Twelve Step recovery programs, participants are urged to make a "faithful and relentless inventory of their wrongs, and where possible to make amends." You might want to journal your way through the confession. I have sometimes written each sentence at the top of a page in my journal and written under the heading, always dating the entry. You could start the journaling on a particular phrase with a prayer, "O God, help me as I reflect on this prayer fragment. Give me courage to face up to the real me—the me you know, the me you love, and the me you forgive. Amen."

We confess . . .
Our self-indulgent appetites and ways, and our
    exploitation of other people,
We confess to you, Lord.

Our anger at our own frustration, and our envy
    of those more fortunate than ourselves,
We confess to you, Lord.

Our intemperate love of worldly goods and
    comforts, and our dishonesty in daily life
    and work,
We confess to you, Lord.[29]

To personalize the prayer, change the pronouns
from the plural to the singular. You can change
the congregational response, "Have mercy on
us, Lord" to "Have mercy on *me*, Lord."

I would recommend that you pray the "Litany of Penitence" found in the Ash Wednesday service in *The Book of Common Prayer* (pp. 267-69). I pray this confession every day during Lent. In actuality, the prayer focuses on the nitty gritty of single adult life. Frankly, it is a tough prayer for me to get through.

However, this prayer can also be prayed at any time during the year. In fact, when you are pondering your New Year's resolutions, or waiting for the bowl games to start, that's a good time to pick up the Prayer Book and pray through these awesome words. Or you might want to pray through this liturgical prayer on your birthday.

28. The Prayer of Thanksgiving ● ● ● ● ● ● ● ● ● ● ● ● ● ● ● ●

Any single adult who stops to think about single adults living in the global "hot spots" or single adults in Third World countries, has a lot for which to say, "Thank you."

"I thank my God every time I remember you, constantly praying with joy in every one of my prayers for all of you."—*Philippians 1:3, 4*

"We prevent God from giving us the great spiritual gifts He has in store for us, because we do not give thanks for daily gifts. . . . We pray for the big things and forget to give thanks for the ordinary, small (and yet really not small) gifts. How can God entrust great things to one who will not thankfully receive from Him the little things?" (Dietrich Bonhoeffer)[30]

I keep a piece of calligraphy on the wall in my study that reads "O Lord, you have given me so much. Now give me one more thing: a grateful heart!" It's so easy to base my attitude about gratitude on my checkbook or net worth, on what I am wearing, or driving.

Years ago, Joni Eareckson-Tada, then a single adult, convinced me that the menu for gratitude was much broader than I realized when she asked, "How would you like to be out on a date and need your bladder bag emptied?" I had never thanked the Lord for the capacity to urinate. Because I do not have a kidney disease and I am not physically challenged, going to the bathroom is a fairly simple process. But if I were physically challenged, that basic need would be more complicated.

"How shall I ever be able to thank God sufficiently?" (Søren Kierkegaard) [31]

In our thanksgivings we put a lot of items under the umbrella with the sweeping statement, "and for all your blessings, Lord, we are grateful." Some things we do not or will not pray about. That is why I love to hear children pray—they have not learned the editing process yet. Most children just pray whatever happens to be on their minds. Prayer is that simple: if you can think about it, you can pray about it. Corrie ten Boom lived out that philosophy; so can you.

"Now, Father, you have heard what we have been talking about. You know the need. We thank you for listening. We thank you for caring. And we trust You to supply us. Hallelujah. Amen." (Corrie ten Boom) [32]

It is a blessing every morning that I lace up my shoes to jog—that I can lace up the shoes and that I can run. It is a blessing every day to be able to eat and digest food. I do not have to worry about my next meal (although I may need to worry about my last meal, if I overate). It is a blessing to be able to think clearly. It is a blessing to be able to read.

Fill in your thanksgivings in the space below:

It is a blessing to _____.

It is a blessing to _____.

It is a blessing to _____.

It is a blessing to _____.

It is a blessing to _____.

What blessing came to mind that you hesitated to write down? See how we self-edit and limit our thanksgivings? "Oh," you might argue, "God knows how grateful I am about that without my specifically mentioning it." Really?

Single adults in this country have been so sheltered from concern about "daily necessities." We expect to turn on a shower and have a stream of clean, safe, hot water come out. How we gripe if we run out of hot water! In many areas of the world, running water is a luxury. In many areas, single adults spend incredible time finding or preparing food. We just drive to a drive-through window (and fume if the line is slow) or pop something in a microwave. When was the last time you have thanked God for the food industry in this country?

"(Imagine being) in this glorious world with grateful hearts—and no one to thank."
(Christina Rossetti) [33]

 Take a moment and think of ten things you have never specifically thanked God for. O God, I have never thanked you for

1. _____.
2. _____.
3. _____.
4. _____.
5. _____.
6. _____.
7. _____.
8. _____.
9. _____.
10. _____.

Ask God to "remind" you of other things you are thankful for. Make some time for a "time out for gratitude." First read Psalm 136. Take a few moments to reflect on what you have read. Pray aloud, "God, would you bring to my mind those gifts for which I have never offered thanks?" Then begin writing them down as they come to mind. If you are a single parent, this is a great family exercise.

"For three things I thank the Lord every day of my life: thanks that he has vouchsafed me knowledge of his works; deep thanks that he has set in my darkness the lamp of faith; deep, deepest thanks that I have another life to look forward to—a life joyous with light and flowers and heavenly song." (Helen Keller) [34]

Or you might do this exercise with a friend. Number one to twenty-five on a sheet of paper. Hand the sheet and a pencil to a friend and have the person repeatedly ask this question of you, "One thing I am thankful for is . . . ?" The repetition jars the brain. When you have identified twenty-five items, trade places. You now ask your friend, "One thing I am thankful for is . . . ?" and write down your friend's responses. Date the list.

Thank you very, very much; my God, thank you.
Give me food today, food for my sustenance every day.
Thank you very, very much." (Desmond Tutu) [35]

Thank the Lord for this re-remembering. Take time with your friend and talk about your lists.

29. Praying the Prayers of Supplication •••••••••

Supplication is more than a pious rendition of a Christmas wish list.
"Ask, and it will be given you."—*Matthew 7:7*

It is tempting to create a Prayer Success Inventory—a way of determining, in our statistically oriented culture, the percentage of our prayers that are successfully answered. I grew up in a tradition with "prayer warriors," individuals who "knew how to pray" or who "knew how to get hold of God." They were supposed to have an inside track when it came to praying. You wanted them "on your side," to "put in a good word."

During my divorce, I turned to some of them, since my prayers for reconciliation did not seem to be doing too well. It was like bringing in specialists or heavy hitters. Divorce was big stakes—no time for amateurs. Despite all my praying and the praying of others, the divorce became final. I did not get my miracle. That little tap of the judge's gavel that ended my marriage, for all practical purposes ended my praying. What good was it to pray? So, for years, I did not pray.

In my doctoral work in spirituality, I had to do intense reading about prayer. I remember the crisis I faced one day in a class discussion on prayer. After a rather spirited discussion on prayer in which I had remained silent, the professor said, "Harold Ivan, you haven't contributed anything on this topic."

"Well," I hesitated, wondering how my honesty would impact my grade or my rapport in the group, "that's because I don't pray . . . very much."

Apparently the professor thought he had not heard me correctly. "What did you say?"

"I said, 'I don't pray.' " I answered softly.

"May I ask why? This is a doctoral program in spirituality."

"Well, when I went through my divorce, I prayed my guts out and nothing happened. Jane still divorced me. So, I just decided, 'Why pray? God, you take care of the world. I will take care of me.'" The silence in the room was incredible. "I know I ought to pray. . . ."

After a reflective moment, the professor asked me, "What are you going to do about it?"

"Well, I'd like some prayer." So, in that classroom, I knelt and my doctoral colleagues gathered around me and prayed for me, that God would give me the ability to pray and to trust. That day changed my spiritual life. While I am still not ready to brag about my batting average in prayer, I have learned that prayer is more about a relationship than about well-formulated verbalizations and "beautiful" prayers.

> "I believe that we pray much more than we realize. We pray in our pain, tears and joy. Our very being is a living prayer reaching out to God in thanksgiving for life itself. Prayer is who we are, not just what we do." (William Dobbels) [36]

Supplication involves two focuses of prayer: intercession, praying for others, and petition, presenting one's own needs. We will focus on intercession in this chapter, and on petition in chapter 30.

> "I do not cease to give thanks for you as I remember you in my prayers." —*Ephesians 1:16*

Intercession is praying for others; a major spiritual discipline in the life of Paul, a single adult. Admittedly, I have had great difficulty praying for others. If God is all knowing and all-caring, then why do I have to "remind" him, for example, that my friend John is ill, dying? That Ann, my single parent friend, has an ex-spouse who thinks alimony and child support are voluntary? Does God have so much on his mind that occasionally it has to be jarred? Is my prayer like tying a string around God's finger so he will not forget? I still don't understand this, but I am learning by doing, by being in an intercessory prayer group and through interceding for my friend, John. Oh, how he wanted to live.

> "Let us remain constant in prayer for one another. Who knows how much protection through God's grace he owes to the intercession of a brother?" (Dietrich Bonhoeffer) [37]

I belong to a congregation that has an active intercessory prayer ministry. On Sunday, communicants fill out little prayer cards, writing down people or situations for which they desire prayer. On Thursday mornings, parishioners gather in the choir loft and go through those cards, praying sometimes for people they do not know.

Sunday after Sunday, I wrote, "Please pray for my friend, John, who is dying."

I do not know who prayed for John or even how they prayed. But it was comforting to me to know that every Thursday morning someone knelt in that sacred space and repeated John's name and reminded the God who deeply loved John that he was dying. I suspect that they also prayed for me—that God would help me "lose" my friend with grace.

In those last weeks, when I knew little to comfort John in our phone chats other than trivia, I reminded him that members of my church were praying for him by name.

I felt so frustrated, 1,500 miles from my dying friend. I kept sending him cards and clippings. I wanted him to know that he was in my thoughts and on my heart. I felt so helpless; all I could do for John was pray.

I finally told John that I felt helpless, that I wished there were something more I can do. "All I can do for you . . ." One of the last things John said to me was, "Tell them to keep praying . . . that helps. I need it."[38]

> "From the moment we wake until we fall asleep, we must commend other people wholly and unreservedly to God and leave them in his hands, and transform our anxiety for them into prayers on their behalf." (Dietrich Bonhoeffer) [39]

My friend John died. I stopped writing his name on the little white cards. I wrote other requests for prayer: for his sister, for his mother, for his close friend Greg, who were all trying to get used to a world without John. And now, there are more names for which I request prayers, because I am at that age where the dying starts picking up speed.

Many mornings I now make my way to that sacred place and accept my cards and kneel at the altar and pray my way through cards that have been assigned me. I remind God of what he already knows: someone is sick, someone is dying. Mostly, I pray for strangers, but then strangers prayed for my friend.

I have also found that in intercessory prayer, things come to mind that I can do to partially answer my prayer. Praying for others—even if they are little "bullet" prayers, "O God help _____" is helpful for the pray-er and the prayee.

> "We never know how God will answer our prayers, but we can expect that He will get us involved in His plan for the answer. If we are true intercessors, we must be ready to take part in God's work on behalf of the people for whom we pray." (Corrie ten Boom) [40]

> "Intercession is the greatest fruit-bearing work that God gives us to do." (Belle Bennett) [41]

Take a moment and think of individuals or situations that need your prayers. Begin by praying, "Lord, thank you for the privilege of praying. Bring to my mind those who need prayer." Pause a moment. Then list the names:

☐ _____   ☐ _____
☐ _____   ☐ _____
☐ _____   ☐ _____

Now take a moment to pray for each one. Ask the Lord what you can do to communicate your concern. Then finish the time by thanking God for the privilege of praying for others.

Another technique is to put the names and needs on 3 x 5 index cards. Then you can use them like flash cards. You are more apt to remember to pray for them this way, or if you write them on a list, than to rely on your memory.

An Intercessory Agenda

On Monday pray for your family.
On Tuesday pray for world leaders.
On Wednesday pray for friends.
On Thursday pray for those who are ill.
On Friday pray for children.
On Saturday pray for your pastor, your church.
On Sunday pray for all of the above.

 Take a moment to pray. Whatever day of the week it is when you read this, pray accordingly.

I have a little notebook marked one through thirty-one. Each number stands for a day of the month. Under each date are names of family members, friends, colleagues, as well as situations to pray for. On months with thirty days, I combine thirty and thirty-one. But it means all of my friends can be specifically prayed for, by name, once a month.

It is helpful to know that 2,000 years ago, on the eve of his arrest and crucifixion, Jesus Christ was thinking of and praying for me. In the NIV, the subheadings of John 17 are, "Jesus Prays for Himself," "Jesus Prays for His Disciples," and "Jesus Prays for All Believers." In his greatest hour of need, Jesus was interceding for those who would believe in him, later. He prayed for us.

"I ask not only on behalf of these, but also on behalf of those who will believe in me through their word, that they may all be one. As you, Father, are in me and I am in you, may they also be in us, so that the world may believe that you have sent me." —John 17:20-21

Paul's letters are sprinkled with his intercessory prayers for others. Take a moment and look up these verses mentioning intercessory prayer:

Romans 1:9
Romans 15:30
Ephesians 1:16
Colossians 4:12
1 Timothy 2:1
2 Timothy 2:1
1 Thessalonians 1:2
Philemon 4, 22

"When I remember you in my prayers, I always thank my God. . . ."—*Philemon 4*

I am impressed that Paul, already a busy man, remembered the people he had met in his travels, some of whom were single adults. Francis Asbury followed the same practice. What impressed you in the citations you selected?

_____

_____

Whom can you be interceding for?

_____	_____	_____	_____
_____	_____	_____	_____
_____	_____	_____	_____
_____	_____	_____	_____

30. Praying Our Petitions ●

By the time I finish praying for me, I don't have time to pray for anyone else.

"Do not worry about anything, but in everything by prayer and supplication with thanksgiving let your requests be made known to God."—*Philippians 4:6*

Prayer must have been difficult for Paul, a single adult. "In every thing . . . let your requests be made known to God" has to be considered alongside his life experiences. Paul:

- ☐ received thrity-nine lashes five times.
- ☐ was beat with rods three times.
- ☐ was stoned one time.
- ☐ was bit by a poisonous snake.
- ☐ was shipwrecked.
- ☐ was in danger from rivers, bandits, Jews, Gentiles, and so on.

He confessed, "We do not want you to be unaware . . . of the affliction we experienced . . . ; for we were so utterly, unbearably crushed that we despaired of life itself. Indeed, we felt that we had received the sentence of death" (2 Corinthians 1:8-9). If Paul prayed before or during some of these things, he surely must have wanted to avoid them. Apparently his prayer success average was not so hot.

Or, perhaps Paul prayed for grace and strength to endure whatever came his way. I have come to believe that God has not promised to protect us from certain things, but to be with us in and through the painful experience. This has become my philosophy of prayer.

There is nothing that is going to happen today that God won't see me through. It may be unpleasant, unfair, and uncomfortable. God will either see me through it or bring enough resources and friends to get me through! I believe this, but most days I hope I won't have to find out how much I believe it.

Many single adults have one item on their prayer agenda: a mate. Their world revolves around a naked ring finger. Some finally stop praying because the dominant prayer of their life has not been answered.

I have always found inspiration in the life of Stella Dysart. In the early thirties, this divorcée went broke drilling for oil in New Mexico. After she laid off employees and scaled back her operations, she stayed in the field, convinced that oil was there. One day a prospector stumbled onto her land and asked, "What are you drilling for?"

"What does it look like?" she retorted. "Should I be looking for something else?" The old prospector shared a hunch with her and they formed an agreement to split anything besides oil that was found.

In 1955 the "struck it rich" Dysart ended up owning a significant portion of the world's *uranium*. She had been in the right place all along, but she had been looking for the wrong resource! She spent the rest of her life sharing her wealth with those investors who had lost money in her oil business in the thirties.

"When you pray, ask for guidance, strength, and inspiration." (Stella Dysart) [42]

What have you been praying for? In the left column, list the priorities of your intentional prayer. In the second space, rank them in order. For example, for many readers, a mate will be #1.

_____   _____

_____   _____

_____   _____

Now that you have thought about your prayers, take another look at Stella's priorities. Do you need to revise your prayer priorities?

"Petition is the act of asking God for the deepest needs of our lives. Jesus said, 'Ask and it shall be given you; seek and you shall find.' Because he instructed us to ask for our needs, pray boldly for them." (Ilona Buzick) [43]

One single adult prayed boldly—a scientist by the name of George Washington Carver. He thought that he could help his people by convincing a group of black farmers to grow peanuts in sufficient quantity that they could corner the market and control prices and reap tremendous economic benefits. Unfortunately, there were problems with the peanuts and the crop could not be sold. Carver was devastated by the experience and felt like a fool. He went off by himself to pray.

"Lord. Why did you create the world?"

"I can't answer that," God answered. "That's too deep for you to comprehend."

"Then, Lord, why did you create man?"

"I can't answer that either. That's too deep for you, too."

"Then, Lord, why did you create *me*?"

"I can't answer that either. That's too deep for you, too."

Exasperated, Carver prayed, "Then tell me, Lord, what in the world am I going to do with all these peanuts?"

And God said, "Now that I can answer." Is it any wonder that George Washington Carver discovered over 300 uses of the peanut, including tires, dyes, plastics, wood stains, powdered milk, and even flour? God used this single adult's inquisitiveness to revolutionize the agricultural economy of the South. It all began with a prayer. I hope you will think about the peanut the next time someone suggests, "You don't have a prayer!"[44]

A wonderful scripture passage becomes the emotional life raft for the single adult to cling to. Paul declared, from firsthand personal experience, "And my God will fully satisfy every need of yours according to his riches in glory in Christ Jesus" (Philippians 4:19). Underline the key phrase in that verse. I hope you marked, "every need."

Unfortunately, a lot of single adults translate "all your wants," which quickly degenerates into a "name it and claim it" mentality, especially for those who use "we ask this in Jesus' name" as an open-sesame word.

Living in a zealously materialistic society, I frequently need to pray for the wisdom to know the difference between wants, needs, and whims, especially since I don't have to discuss my consumerism with a spouse. I need to be spiritually wise enough not to see God as a benevolent Santa Claus, zealously showering us with the goodies, or in the rawest sense "the loot." Sometimes, I have to be reminded that "no" or "later" are in my best spiritual interests. I also need to know that I don't prove my Christian faith by the brand labels of what I drive, own, or wear. The notion, "Nothing's too good for a child of the King," is misguided greed.

"God loves to hear us tell him what a sense our souls have of our own particular necessities and troubles. He loves to hear us complain before him, when we are under any pressures from his hand, or when we stand in need of mercies of any kind." (Isaac Watts) [45]

It should be noted that *complain* did not have a negative connotation in Watts's day.

Make "not my will but thine" a reality in my life.

"Yet not what I want, but what you want."
—Mark 14:36

"It's hard to hate someone for whom you are praying." That's what one of my friends said in talking about her decision to pray for the man who raped her one Easter weekend when she was a single parent. Pray for a rapist? You have got to be kidding! Yet, her decision may be why she has been so effective in ministering to thousands of single parents.

Whom do you dislike that you will not pray for them?
- [ ] *An ex-spouse*
- [ ] *Someone who dumped you*
- [ ] *Someone who took advantage of you sexually*
- [ ] *Someone who sabotaged your chance for a workplace promotion*
- [ ] *A former boss*
- [ ] *An ex-friend who betrayed your confidence*
- [ ] *Your parents*

Write in those names—or initials—below:

Names	*Their offenses*
_____	_____
_____	_____
_____	_____

God, how do I talk to you about these people?

In some of the psalms I find a "kill 'em" or "make 'em pay, Lord" vengeance. This is particularly demonstrated in Psalm 109: "May his children be orphans, and his wife a widow. May his children wander about and beg; may they be driven out of the ruins they inhabit. . . . May there be no one to do him a kindness" (vv. 9-12).

Sometimes we need to pray the prayer of relinquishment. One of the greatest examples of this was Corrie ten Boom, who earned her place in a Nazi concentration camp during World War II by hiding Jews in her home; her sister Betsie died in Ravensbrook while Corrie was released due to a clerical error. Before the war, Corrie had been in love with a young theological student, Karel; she assumed they would marry and minister together. Then one day Karel came to her home and introduced her to his fiancée. Corrie was devastated and fled to the safety of her bedroom. Eventually her father came to her, his heart impacted too, by her loss.

But this was a hurt no blanket could shut out, and suddenly I was afraid of what Father would say. Afraid he would say, "There will be someone else soon," and that forever afterward this untruth would lie between us. For in some deep part of me I knew already there would not—soon or ever—be anyone else.[46]

Eventually this brokenhearted young woman prayed, "Lord, I give to You the way I feel about Karel, my thoughts about our future—oh, You know! Give me Your way of seeing Karel instead. Help me to love him that way. That much."[48]

In the dark Casper ten Boom spoke, reminding his daughter that while love is the strongest force in the world, "When it's blocked that means pain. There are two things that we can do when this happens. We can kill the love so that it stops hurting. But then, of course, part of us dies too. Or, Corrie, we can ask God to open up another route for that love to travel."[47]

The prayer of relinquishment is similar to the prayer of Stephen—the church's first martyr—"Lord Jesus, receive my spirit" (Acts 7:59).

"Oh," you protest, "I don't want to let go—at least, not quite yet—of some of the anger or my desire for revenge."

Many single parents struggle because of their ex-spouse can hurt them again, or hurt or disappoint their children.

How do we deal with the fact that an ex-spouse or someone we once loved is getting married?

How do we let go of the fact that the "other party" who won over an ex-spouse's affections has married him/her, and now they have a beautiful new baby, a new home, x, y, and/or z?

How do we relinquish our claim checks for justice—especially when we feel that the guilty one got away, scot-free? Single adults have the capacity to "stage" all kinds of miseries for those who have hurt them—deep in the arena called imagination.

"On all my expeditions prayer made me stronger morally and mentally than my nonpraying companions. It gave me confidence. Without prayer I doubt that I could have endured the flourishing of spears when they were but half a dozen paces from me. I know that when I have called I have been answered, strengthened, assisted." (Sir Henry Stanley)[49]

I consider Jesus praying so intensely on the night of Judas's betrayal, that "his sweat became like great drops of blood" (Luke 22:44). I detect his reluctant relinquishment evolving.

Prayer 1: "My Father, if it is possible, let this cup pass from me; yet not what I want but what you want" (Matthew 26:39).

What is the key phrase in this first prayer?

_____

Then after an interlude when he had to wake up his three snoozing friends, the ones he had chosen to be with him in his agony, the ones he had told, "My soul is overwhelmed with sorrow," he said, "The spirit indeed is willing, but the flesh is weak" (Matthew 26:41). I have always thought those words were to admonish the disciples for falling asleep; now, I think this was a confession of Jesus' vulnerability, "My spirit is willing, but my body is weak." Jesus returned to prayer, his buddies resumed their nap.

Prayer 2: "My Father, if this cannot pass unless I drink it, your will be done" (Matthew 26:42).

What is the key phrase in this second prayer?

_____

Again Jesus woke up his friends. Then he returned and repeated Prayer 2.

I don't think Jesus waltzed to the cross. I don't think he wanted to die. But in the Mount of Olives, he relinquished his own plans and submitted to God's.

The fact that Jesus' struggle in prayer is mentioned in Matthew 26:36-46, Mark 13:32-42, and Luke 22:39-46 is significant. The Lord knew that his example of struggling in prayer would, centuries later, encourage us in our struggling moments. The author of Hebrews observed, "For we do not have a high priest who is unable to sympathize with our weaknesses, but we have one who in every respect has been tested as we are, yet without sin" (Hebrews 4:15). The result, "Let us then therefore approach the throne of grace with boldness, so that we may receive mercy and find grace to help in time of need" (v. 16). So, in those moments we pray, "Lord, isn't it possible for you to prevent this divorce? To rescue this relationship? Lord, isn't there something you can do about _____?" we find the courage to let go of our plans and wishes. "Not my will but thine."

Catherine Marshall learned relinquishment through her own illness and through the death of her husband, chaplain of the U.S. Senate, Peter Marshall, that "Jesus' prayer in the Garden of Gethsemane is a pattern for us."

Prayer of Relinquishment

Lord, this day in this particular situation given the circumstances as I understand them I pray for wisdom to know your will, courage to do your will, strength to live with your will. But I need you to remind me your will is always for my good. Amen.

Single adults still have "wrestlings" in prayer, when we focus intensely on the "*if* it is possible" perspective. We hope friends are praying in tandem with us, but then again, like Jesus, we may be praying "Lone Ranger" style. Sometimes, we have to pray the "want to" prayer. "Help me, Lord, come to the place, of wanting your will, not mine." Or, as one single prayed, "Help my want-to, want to." The unrelinquished in my life keeps me looking in my rearview mirror to my past, rather than through my windshield into my future. Perhaps your single season and your longings for spiritual growth are being hampered by your links to the past.

Spend a few moments reading Psalm 139:23-24:

"Search me, O God, and know my heart; test me and know my thoughts. See if there is any wicked way in me, and lead me in the way everlasting."

What in my life, such as claim checks, desires for revenge, settling the scores, could fit into the phrase "any wicked way"?

_____

_____

_____

Lord, you know me. Thoroughly. Too thoroughly. It's easy to read the Psalmist's words, "Search and know, test and know." It's hard to pray them. I'm pretending that you don't know about _____. Or that you won't get too close to discover _____. I need to let go of this, Lord. I know I do. You know I do. But I can't, not just yet. Help me relinquish _____. And Lord, once I have relinquished it, can you give me the courage to keep on relinquishing it? Otherwise I'll resuscitate it. Give me the courage to do the right thing. Lead me in the way everlasting. Amen.

> Almighty and eternal God, so draw our hearts to *thee*, so guide our minds, so fill our imaginations, so control our wills, that we may be wholly *thine*, utterly dedicated *unto thee*; and then use us, we pray *thee*, as *thou wilt*, and always to *thy* glory and the welfare of *thy* people; through our Lord and Savior Jesus Christ. *Amen.*[50]

The Book of Common Prayer again offers a jump starter for praying the prayer of relinquishment:

That's relinquishing. What would happen if single adults prayed that prayer for thirty days? Are you willing to find out?

32. Praying Centering Prayer ••••••••••••••••••

> Centering prayer is the Christian's shorthand for "Help."
>
> "Pray in the Spirit at all times in every prayer and supplication." —*Ephesians 6:18*

"Oh, I know that as a believer I ought to pray. And I want to pray. It's just when I get around to praying my mind wanders, the phone rings, the apartment maintenance man starts mowing, the guy in the next apartment 'blasts' me with his new rock CD, or my children interrupt. I cannot concentrate." When Jesus' disciples asked, "Teach us to pray," they captured our heart cry. It is tempting to want a technique, a string of one, two, threes or do this and presto! Results! Praying that counts!

Some single adults find centering prayer helpful. They set aside twenty minutes, two times a day. Thomas Keating, a recognized teacher of centering prayer, offers these suggestions for starting.

☐ Choose a sacred word as a "symbol of your intention to consent to God's presence." Words frequently chosen include names for God, *Abba* (father), *Jesu* (Jesus), *Kyrie* (Lord), or characteristics of God: *silence, peace, shalom, mercy,* or *grace.*

> Can you think of a word that you could use? _____

☐ Sit comfortably, close your eyes, breathe deeply. Choose the word. Then, Keating says, "introduce the sacred word inwardly and gently as if laying a feather on a piece of absorbent cotton."[51]

☐ When thoughts start demanding your attention, repeat the sacred word. Keating notes that "thoughts" include feelings, images, memories, reflections, or commentaries. Don't chastise yourself if the thoughts persist like impatient two-year-olds. Simply repeat the sacred word.

☐ As the prayer time draws to a close, sit quietly for a couple of minutes and slowly become more aware of your surroundings.

Initially, you may want to use a timer—rather than to keep looking at a watch or clock. Yes, the time will go very slowly at first, but stay with it. You will be tempted to snarl, "I can't do this!" I thought the same thing when I started practicing centering prayer. You will be stunned by the number of things that "pop" into your mind. Initially, I sat with a small notebook and wrote down the stream of "things to do" demanding my attention and interrupting my concentration. But eventually persistence will win out; the discipline will take. You will be stunned by the calm you feel and by the amount of time that has gone by.

Hot Fudge! Don't you dare think of a hot fudge sundae while reading this section. Just put it out of your mind. But now you are thinking about it. Why? Because you are trying *not* to think about it. Sometimes, I just say, "Okay, I'll think about that at 10 A.M." Sometimes bizarre thoughts wander through to distract my prayer. Where did that come from? Just let them pass.

It will be helpful to have a brief drink of water, to go to the bathroom, and so forth, before doing centering prayer. Legitimate body needs are distracting. I have found making a place to pray adds to my resolve. Also, I pay attention to posture and breathing. If I don't get enough oxygen, I'll go to sleep. I have also found that I have to do my centering prayer first thing in the morning. If I jog first, I am wired. If I have coffee, I am wired. If I read some devotional commentary, my mind rehashes what I just read. Certainly, there is a place for devotional reading, but not now. Centering prayer is my launch pad for the day. When I don't do it, I soon know it.

How to start? I started with five minutes and added time.

You may have to set aside a deep myth. You may tend to think of prayer as words, language, and that quiet does not count, that real prayer means getting on your knees and speaking.

Thomas Keating explains:

The root of prayer is interior silence. We may think of prayer as thoughts or feelings expressed in words. But this is only one expression. Deep prayer is the laying aside of all thoughts. It is the opening of mind and heart, body and feelings—our whole being—to God, the Ultimate Mystery, beyond words, thoughts or emotions.[53]

You may honestly protest, "I am a single parent. I don't have time for two twenty-minute periods. I hit the ground running in the morning and go until I drop at night. By the time I get the kids in bed, I'm wiped out!" Well do you have time for two ten-minute periods? Two fives?

> **When will be a good time and place for you to start learning centering prayer?**
>
> Time: _____
>
> Place: _____

"So many single adults think that the most important thing, the thing he must concentrate upon, is that God should hear what he is praying for. Yet in the true, eternal sense it is just the reverse: the true relation in prayer is not when God hears what is prayed for, but when the person (single adult) continues to pray until he is the one who hears, who hears what God wills. The 'immediate' person, therefore, . . . makes demands in his prayers; the true man of prayer only (listens)." (Søren Kierkegaard) [54]

Maybe Desmond Tutu said it best: "Our relationship with God is a love affair and ultimately the greatest joy is just to be with the Beloved, to drink in the beauty of the Beloved in a silence that will become more and more wordless and imageless—the silence of just being together."[55]

33. Praying the Mirror Prayer ●●●●●●●●●●●●●●●●●

"Prayer changes things." Ah, what a lovely cliché!

"But whenever you pray, go into your room and shut the door and pray to your Father who is in secret."—*Matthew 6:6*

One of the top ten clichés on prayer, if Letterman were so inclined, is "Prayer changes things." I have learned that prayer does not always change things, but prayer changes me and my attitudes about things.

All of us have something about our bodies we wish we could change, to make us more sexually attractive. For some, middle age has accelerated the process. Indeed, some of us say the most outrageous things to ourselves: "No wonder you're single. Just look at you!"

The mirror prayer is a challenge. Jesus can identify with some of our struggles. Scripture reports, "He had no form or majesty that we should look at him, nothing in his appearance that we should desire him" (Isaiah 53:2). Maybe that's a verse to meditate on before we launch the next verbal blitzkrieg on ourselves or on some particular body part that makes us uncomfortable.

We live in a body-centric culture. We all know about the thin, the beautiful, the "with it" people. You won't find them munching popcorn, watching a video alone on Saturday night. Some of us have concluded, "If only I could change _____, then I would be dating or married." This notion keeps the appointment books of plastic surgeons and psychologists filled.

This body-fixated culture constantly reminds us of our inadequacies: "Your breasts are too big/too small. Your penis is too small. Your buttocks are too big. Your abdomen protrudes. Your gut hangs over your belt!" Many of us would die before we would admit such feelings of inadequacy to a friend—but deep in the interior, the battle rages. That's one reason single adults drag themselves to health clubs and gyms. "Gotta do something about _____!" Then we unleash our harsh criticism on ourselves: "Just look at you. Who would want *you!* No wonder you are single!" Some of us ignore our bodies; some of us abuse our bodies. So instead of dieting or exercising, we gain more weight. Or we hide our annoying body part under layers of clothing.

Scriven urged us to bring "everything" to God in prayer. He also said to bring not just our sins but also "our griefs" to God in prayer. Remembering that God already knows about our well-rehearsed negative attitudes, some of us need to add the mirrored praying to our repertoire.

I tricked you! Are you uncomfortable because I left twice as many spaces for positive comments than for negatives? Some of us had difficulty finding *anything* about our body we like or accept. Unfortunately, our body hears every insult we heap!

Now go back and redo the previous exercise. First, recite Psalm 139:14 three times. As you write down something you like, repeat the psalm phrase.

"I praise you, for I am fearfully and wonderfully made. Wonderful are your works."
—Psalm 139:14

What about your body underscores the psalmist's declaration? _____

Now, focus on the biggest positive. Thank the Lord for that body reality. "O Lord, I feel a little strange doing this, but I want to thank you for my _____.

When I see _____ I feel _____.

I thank you for a healthy body. Give me a healthy attitude toward my body, the temple of your Holy Spirit."

If our bodies are temples of the Holy Spirit, as Paul declared in 1 Corinthians 6:19 and 2 Corinthians 6:16, why do we say such harsh things about parts of those temples? _____

Breathe deeply, three or four times. Now focus on the biggest negative. Tell the Lord how you feel. "O Lord, I feel a little strange doing this, but you already know how I feel about my _____.

When I look at my _____

I feel _____.

I know you made me. Help me change this if I can: if I can't help me have the strength to change my attitude toward my _____."

One way single adults are spiritually defeated is by coveting the anatomy of another. In the Ten Commandments, a portion of the last commandment gets shortchanged. We know we should not covet our neighbor's house or wife or manservant or ox/donkey. But what about the last section, "Or *anything* that belongs to your neighbor" (Exodus 20:17)? What have you coveted that "belongs" to your neighbor?

We live singly in such a body/beauty-fixated culture, we focus primarily on the body and ignore the soul. When Samuel scrutinized the sons of Jesse for a potential king, he initially considered the older sons. But the Lord whispered, "Do not look on his appearance or the height of his stature, . . . for the LORD does not see as mortals see; they look on the outward appearance, but the LORD looks on the heart" (1 Samuel 16:7).

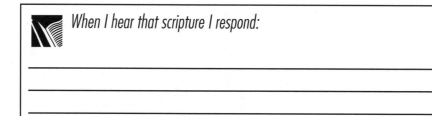

When I hear that scripture I respond:

_____

_____

_____

Sadly, our single adult world overemphasizes the exterior; it's the equivalent of choosing a frozen dinner because the box is so attractive.

Charlotte Elliott well understood how singleness and body image and attitudes interact. When asked by evangelist Cesar Melan if she was a Christian, she replied, "If no man would want me, why would Jesus want me?" Melan suggested that she come to Jesus "just as you are." Later Elliott wrote the powerful words that became the hymn, "Just as I Am."

"Just as I am, though tossed about, With many a conflict, many a doubt, Fightings and fears within, without, O Lamb of God, I come, I come." (Charlotte Elliott) [56]

Miss Elliott's hymn is commonly used as a song of invitation to salvation or spiritual renewal. However, it is also a powerful invitation to discipleship and the devotional life. I must come to Jesus *as I am* and I bring all of me that makes up my "I am." We, too, come bringing our fightings, our abusive talk, and treatment of our bodies and the bodies of others.

34. Praying Our Sexuality ●●●●●●●●●●●●●●●●●●●

For many single adults, the only taboo in prayer is mentioning their sexuality.

"Or do you not know that . . . you are not your own? For you were bought with a price; therefore glorify God in your body."
—1 Corinthians 6:19-20

David nervously fidgeted; I waited for his question. "Well," he said, taking a deep breath, "have you ever, well, ah, you know, like on a Saturday night, you're all worked up, you know, and like, well, you're feeling. . . ." He paused.

"Horny?" I said softly.

"Yeah. How do you know that word?" he asked.

"We used it when we came down the gangplank from the *Mayflower* at Plymouth Rock, 'Boy, am I horny!' "

"Yeah, well, like what do you do about it?"

"Have you ever thought of talking to God about it?" I asked.

"To God?" he whispered, stunned. "You can't talk to God about sex! What would he think?"

"David, he already knows."

"Oh, no!" he covered his face with his hands. "I'm in big trouble!"

Amazingly, many single adults cannot imagine talking to God about their sexual desires, needs, longings, expressions. Some have never been able to talk to anyone about them. They sing, "What a friend we have in Jesus," without considering that the writer's "everything to God in prayer" includes sexuality. The consequence is the same, "O what peace we often forfeit, o what needless pain we bear."

Some of us have been so negatively conditioned that anything sexual *must* be sinful. Some single adults feel as guilty about sexual drives and needs as about sexual behavior. Some seek to deny their sexual needs through prayer. One single woman told me that she had no sexual temptation. "Why?" I asked.

"Well, I gave my sexual drive to God."

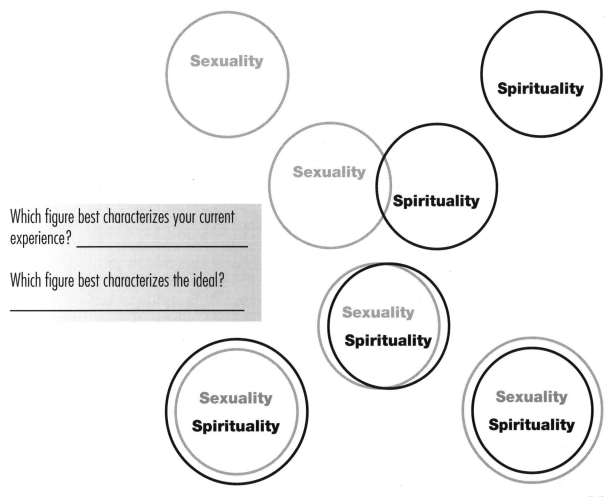

Which figure best characterizes your current experience? _____

Which figure best characterizes the ideal?
_____

In what ways do I honor God with my body:

_____

_____

_____

"Lord, I want to belong to You with my body, soul, and mind. I claim your victory, Lord Jesus, over that wound which is hurting me. Let Your victory be demonstrated in my sex life." (Corrie ten Boom) [57]

Paul knew a few things about sexuality; this single adult strongly declared that sex is for expression between husband and wife. To single adults in the church at Corinth, he wrote, "You are not your own; you were bought at a price. Therefore," he concluded, "glorify God with your body." Centuries ago, single adults were counseled, "Get thee to a nunnery!" Somehow, many single adults thought they could leave their sexuality at the door of the convent or monastery. There, they reasoned, they would be immune from temptation. But monks have told me they have discovered that they can't run away from their sexuality.

Some single adults regard sexual behavior and spirituality as mutually exclusive. So, when they are sexually active, they do not pray or practice devotional life. Like Augustine they pray, "Lord make me pure . . . but not yet."

One way we can honor God is by praying for grace to "help in our time of need," in our times of sexual doubting, or confusion, or temptation—when we toy with compromising our sexual decisions. Paul wrote, "Do not worry about anything." "Anything" includes our sexuality! Paul continued, "But in everything by prayer and supplication with thanksgiving, let your requests be made known to God" (Philippians 4:6). *"With thanksgiving?"* I think it is essential to be thankful for our sexual capacity. Thankful to the Creator for creating such a gift as sexuality-our maleness, our femaleness. Paul addressed the issue of sexual expression by noting that some individuals "worshiped and served the creature" like sexuality "rather than the Creator" (Romans 1:25). John Spong offers sound advice, "So, in our prayers we roam the edges of our human experience and lift it to God without neglecting our own deepest and most personal concerns."[58]

Unfortunately, some have become convinced that a single adult who is "spiritual" has a teflon-like coating, so sexual temptations are easily sidestepped. That has led some to a spiritual pride: *"I* can do all things through Christ who strengths *me."* Their *I* is definitely in neon. But "through Christ" is Paul's intended emphasis.

It is natural to feel the "want to" blues. Spirituality does not deplete your hormones; it just equips you to discipline them.

O God, you know all things, you know all secrets, nothing is hidden from you. Nothing! No thing. So, you know, don't you? You know that my "no" tonight was not enthusiastic. "No" was forced across my lips. I didn't want to say no. I wanted to. Three words captured the situation: I wanted to. . . . Who ever heard of a single saying no? What would have been so wrong expressing a little love? Who would have ever known? One small thing: I don't feel like telling anyone, let alone bragging that I said no. I made it through, this time, by the skin of my teeth and a two-letter word: No. Only you know, so well, that I wanted—oh how I *wanted*—to say "Yes!" God, it is so tempting as a single adult to want what I want, to want what someone wants to share with me. God, sometimes, it is so difficult to want what you want for me. Amen.

If I believe I am entitled to sexual expression, then it is easy to perceive God as a spoil-sport. However, if I see sexual capacity as a gift from God, then I understand the boundaries God uses to frame sexuality for my good. I see it much like endowment gifts to institutions. When I gave money to endow a scholarship fund in memory of a friend and my father, I placed one little "string" on the money. As the giver of the gift I had every right to restrict its use. The money can only be used for scholarships for theological students. God has a right to declare restrictions on the incredible sexual endowment given to us.

Bishop Tutu said correctly, "Nothing is insignificant for God that is important to us."[59]

35. Praying the Psalms ●

The book of Psalms was the original prayer book.

"Sing psalms and hymns and spiritual songs among yourselves." —*Ephesians 5:19*

When I suggested to a friend going through a divorce that she pray she snapped, "I can't!" I recalled that period of my life. "Well, then, pray the prayers of others." Such as the psalmists. I learned the value of the Psalms as a prayer book during one visit to a monastery. Several times a day the monks gathered to pray the Psalms, sometimes singing, sometimes chanting. Each month, they worked their way through the book of Psalms. The sound of those psalms being sung in that vast basilica is an incredible memory.

In you, O LORD, I seek refuge; do not let me ever be put to shame; in your righteousness deliver me.

Incline your ear to me; rescue me speedily. Be a rock of refuge for me, a strong fortress to save me. You are indeed my rock and my fortress, for your name's sake lead me and guide me, take me out of the net that is hidden for me, for you are my refuge. Into your hand I commit my spirit; you have redeemed me, O LORD, faithful God (Psalm 31:1-5).

Indeed, one phrase of that psalm has become a stand-by-itself prayer, *"Into your hands I commit my spirit."* I have prayed that prayer a few times myself. When Stephen was being martyred by stoning, certainly no kumbaya-type experience, his death being witnessed and "approved" by a single adult named Saul, Stephen prayed this psalm-prayer, "Lord Jesus, receive my spirit." If I had been the one being stoned to death, I would have been calling down the vengeance of heaven: "Get 'em, Lord." But not Stephen. Perhaps that calming psalm, one he had prayed numerous times before as an observant Jew, led him to add, "Lord, do not hold this sin against them" (Acts 7:60).

When you don't know what or how to pray, do what Christians have done for two thousand years—turn to the book of Psalms:

Give ear to my words, O LORD; give heed to my sighing. Listen to the sound of my cry, my King and my God, for to you I pray (5:1-2);

O LORD my God, in you I take refuge; save me from all my pursuers and deliver me (7:1);

O LORD, our Sovereign, how majestic is your name in all the earth (8:1).

The first and last of these psalms, and many others, have been adapted into contemporary choruses. By learning these choruses we are learning the psalms. Many times when we cannot reach for the Bible, the psalms will reach for us.

Some of the Psalms are heavy. They are prayers composed by people in tough places:

Why, O LORD, do you stand far off? Why do you hide yourself in times of trouble? (10:1)

or

My God, my God, why have you forsaken me? Why are you so far from helping me, from the words of my groaning? O my God, I cry out by day, but you do not answer, and by night, but find no rest. (22:1-2)

Paraphrasing the current cliché, I respond, "Been there, felt that way!" Or "Been there, prayed that." But it dawned on me early one morning, meditating on Psalm 22, that Jesus had prayed a portion of this prayer. As he hung between earth and heaven, "Jesus cried with a loud voice." Yes, but what did he say? "My God, my God, why have you forsaken me?" (Matthew 27:46). It helps me to know that Jesus asked the why question. I think of that whenever someone tries to unspiritualize me for my current why questions. It also helps me to know that Jesus prayed "with a loud voice."

Go through the Psalms with a marker and highlight the phrases that speak to you.

"Protect me, O God" (16:1).
"He guards the lives of his faithful [ones]" (97:10).
"He lifts the needy from the ash heap" (113:7).
"I am yours; save me" (119:94).

Many a sleepless night, after one of "those" kinds of days, I have recalled Psalm 3:5-6:

> I lie down and sleep; I wake again, for the LORD sustains me. I am not afraid of ten thousands of people who have set themselves against me all around.

While I have never had "thousands of people" against me, I have had a couple of people try to make my life miserable. So, I remind myself that if the psalmist could sleep in God's care with "thousands" wanting to do him in, I can sleep too.

The benefit of having marked the psalms is that in those moments when I am too anxious, too tired, too angry to be creative, I can pick up my Bible and begin letting my eyes roam the pages of the psalms, like radar driven to the verses I have marked. I have found this to be incredibly calming and assuring. In some cases, I have been captured by a particular phrase and have paused there. In my Bible, I have written in dates when a particular verse spoke to me. They serve as reminders later when I am doubting that God is going to help me. Sometimes, I cannot remember the circumstances, the details, but I can remember the faithfulness. And that becomes that seed of trust that God will work now.

Finally, you can pray Psalm 23; you may already have it memorized. I personalize it, changing the pronouns: "Lord, you are *my* shepherd. I shall not want. You lead me beside still waters. You restore my soul." Other Psalms can be prayed in the same manner. Pray the psalms.

36. Praying the Hymnal ● ● ● ● ● ● ● ● ● ● ● ● ● ● ● ● ● ● ●

A hymnal is a repository of some of the greatest prayers ever prayed.

"As you sing psalms and hymns and spiritual songs among yourselves, singing and making melody to the Lord in your hearts, giving thanks to God the Father at all times and for everything in the name of our Lord Jesus Christ." —*Ephesians 5:19-20*

In the last decade, choruses have gained in popularity in the Christian community, with many churches dismissing the hymnal as archaic. However, individuals committed to spiritual formation know the importance of the hymnal. The wiser approach is a balanced blending of hymns and choruses.

In the hymnal, for example, we find a gamut of expressions and emotions summarizing how God's people cry out for help, giving glory to his name, plead for Christian unity, celebrate his birth, crucifixion, and resurrection from the dead.[60]

I recommend that you take a hymnal and pray some of the hymns as a prayer. You might want to check in a thrift shop or used books bookstore for older hymnals. Start with, "O God Our Help in Ages Past."

O God, Our Help in Ages Past

O God, our help in ages past, our hope for
  years to come,
Our shelter from the stormy blast, and our
  eternal home.

Under the shadow of thy throne, still may we
  dwell secure;
Sufficient is thine arm alone, and our defense is
  sure.

O God, our help in ages past, our hope for
  years to come,
Be thou our guide while life shall last, and our
  eternal home.[61]

How to pray a hymn:

1. Ask God to help you reflect on the hymn lyrics.

2. Read through the entire hymn slowly. Then sing it.

3. Pray the words slowly, substituting first person singular pronouns for third person pausing at the end of each line.

4. Pray: "God, what would you have me hear in these words?"

5. Take the time to journal a response.

6. Thank the Lord for this time.

Other Watts hymns you might pray are "When I Survey the Wondrous Cross," "Come, Holy Spirit, Heavenly Dove," or "I Sing the Almighty Power of God." It might interest you to know that Watts remained a bachelor after the woman he loved told him, "O, Isaac, you are so short! I could never marry you."

Take My Life and Let It Be

Take my life, and let it be Consecrated, Lord, to thee.

Take my moments and my days; Let them flow in ceaseless praise.

Take my will, and make it thine; It shall be no longer mine.

Take my heart, it is thine own; It shall be thy royal throne.[62]

Create a prayer paraphrasing Havergal's words or thought.

Take my singleness and . . .

_____

_____

_____

Other Havergal hymns you might appreciate are "Lord, Speak to Me, That I May Speak," and "Like a River Glorious." Or, you may want to spend time praying Adelaide Pollard's "Have Thine Own Way, Lord."

Many songs can be as easily prayed as sung. Sometimes, it may be as simple as listening in our memories to one of the black spirituals:

> Lord, I want to be a Christian in my heart, in my heart;
> Lord, I want to be a Christian in my heart.
> Lord, I want to be more loving . . .
> Lord, I want to be like Jesus . . .

Or it may mean creating a verse as we sing/pray: Lord, I want to be more Christian in my singleness, in my singleness;
Lord, I want to be more Christian, in my singleness.

Take a moment and reflect on this spiritual. Sing or hum it through. Now, let your creativity flow. Write a verse below:

Lord, I want to be a Christian in my

_____

_____.

It is good to keep a hymnal close to your Bible ready for use in your devotional times. As you do, you will be in the line of millions who have prayed these books above all others, except the Bible.

Here are other hymns that can be prayed:

"Fairest Lord Jesus," "Jesus, The Very Thought of Thee," "Be Thou My Vision," "Guide Me, O Thou Great Jehovah," "Great Is Thy Faithfulness," "Breathe on Me," "Dear Lord and Father of Mankind," "Savior, Like a Shepherd Lead Us," "Come, Thou Fount of Every Blessing," "Spirit of the Living God," "Spirit of God, Descend Upon My Heart," "Abide With Me," "Jesus, Lover of My Soul," "Come Thou Almighty King," and "My Jesus, I Love Thee."

37. Praying the Prayers of Jesus and Paul • • • • • • • • •

What better models for prayer could we have than these two single adults?

"Lord, teach us to pray, as John taught his disciples." — *Luke 11:1*

Unfortunately, we do not have many examples of more personal prayers of Jesus. If we did I suspect they would be lengthy, since he often spent the night in prayer. Perhaps the same is true of Paul. However, we do have examples of their public prayers.

Prayers of Jesus	*Prayers of Paul*
Matthew 6:9*b*-13	Acts 22:10
Luke 10:21*b*-22	1 Thessalonians 3:11-13
John 11:41*b*-42	2 Thessalonians 2:16-17
John 12:27-28	Romans 11:33-36
John 17	2 Corinthians 1:3-5
Mark 14:36	2 Corinthians 13:14
Luke 23:34	Galatians 1:3-4
Mark 15:34	Philippians 1:3-11
Luke 23:46	Ephesians 1:3-10
	Ephesians 3:14-20
	Colossians 1:9-12
	1 Timothy 6:15*b*-16

As I read these prayers, I remind myself that they were prayed by single adults. Paris Donehoo approached this issue in his book, *Prayer in the Life of Jesus*, in which he states that Jesus "told us to pray before he knew the need of it himself. He felt the tug of communion with the Father and knew what it could do for him. In short, when Jesus prayed he prayed as one of us. . . . When he prayed, it was the same cry for help that stretches our souls. . . . He was the Son of God, but he prayed as the Son of man."[63]

Jesus' prayers that we can pray:

- [ ] "Father, I thank you for having heard me" (John 11:41).
- [ ] "Abba, Father, for you all things are possible; Remove this cup (burden or pain or singleness and so forth) from me; yet, not what I want, but what you want" (Mark 14:36).
- [ ] "Father, forgive them; for they do not know what they are doing" (Luke 23:34).
- [ ] "My God, my God, why have you forsaken me?" (Mark 15:34).
- [ ] "Father, into your hands I commend my spirit" (Luke 23:46).
  Or this simple prayer from Paul:
- [ ] "What am I to do, Lord?" (Acts 22:10).

Single adults can also adapt the prayers of Paul by changing a pronoun or being creative. Study the original and the altered NIV versions of 1 Thessalonians 5:23 and Hebrews 13:20-21 below.

---

1 Thessalonians 5:23

Original Version	**Altered Version**
May God himself, the God of peace sanctify you through and through, May your whole spirit, soul and body, be kept blameless at the coming of our Lord Jesus Christ.	May God himself, the God of peace sanctify *me* through and through. May *my* whole spirit, soul and body, be kept blameless at the coming of the Lord Jesus Christ.

Hebrews 13:20-21

Original Version	**Altered Version**
May the God of peace who through the blood of the eternal covenant brought back from the dead our Lord Jesus, that great Shepherd of the sheep, equip you with everything good for doing his will, and may he work in us what is pleasing to him, through Jesus Christ; to whom be glory for ever and ever.	God of peace, who brought back from the dead our Lord Jesus, the great Shepherd of the sheep, equip me with everything good for doing your will, and work in me what is pleasing to you, through Jesus Christ; to whom be glory for ever and ever. Amen.

Jesus knew two thousand years ago that I was going to struggle with this question (of prayer) and he prepared an answer for me. That's extremely comforting for me to know.[64]

Jesus anticipated our struggles with prayer! That's why it is impossible to "wear out our welcome" in prayer. And we will never hear, "It's about time I heard from you!"

"Ceaseless prayer is not a matter of saying prayers but, again, of conversing with God as our most intimate Friend. Then we cannot help but live in His presence, either acknowledging our nearness verbally or in silent adoration." (Susan Muto)[65]

Prayer offers no immunity from the harsh realities of life. After all, bad things happen to good single adults, to paraphrase Rabbi Harold Kushner's bestseller. It is tempting to see prayer as a type of insurance, a hedge against evil. Prayer does not ensure any of us safety; it does invite God into the midst of our circumstances.

"God's stated intention is to be with us through every crisis, not so much as protection but as guide. A daily prayer time has been the best way for me to keep that guide in sight. But when prayer doesn't seem to help, I simply trust I'm God's." (Chris Glasser)[66]

I found these words by Chris Glaser shocking until I had time to give them some serious reflection.

38. Praying the Prayers of Others • • • • • • • • • • • • • •

 Sometimes we need a "jump start" to prayer.

"First of all, I urge that supplications, prayers, intercessions, and thanksgivings be made for everyone."—*1 Timothy 2:1*

If you drive an older car like I do, there will be moments you need the services of a tow truck. This past Thanksgiving I sat fuming because my car would not start; yet I was glad to pay the tow truck driver for a jump start. I have come to think of praying the prayers of others as a spiritual jump start. I am part of a spiritual community that uses *The Book of Common Prayer*, but I grew up in a tradition that engaged only in spontaneous praying. Written prayers were a no-no! Quite a pilgrimage, but I know the moment the pilgrimage became serious. I was in Key West on vacation and on Thanksgiving I attended an Episcopal church. Trying to follow the service was rather complicated, but a phrase from the Thanksgivings section of the prayer book literally took me hostage: "We thank you for setting us at tasks which demand our best efforts, and for leading us to accomplishments which satisfy and delight us."

I qualified as a "yuppie," and that prayer sounded just right to me—rather American, the success-thinker's prayer. But the congregation kept praying: "We thank you also for those disappointments and failures that lead us to acknowledge our dependence on you alone."[67]

Whew! I got lost after that. I re-read those words over and over. Weeks later, I kept trying to remember that prayer and could not get it right. So, I walked into an Episcopal church in my neighborhood and asked to photocopy that prayer. I noticed they had prayer books for sale so I bought one. One of the ministers said, "Come back and pray *with us* sometime. We have lots of good prayers."

The Book of Common Prayer has become a faithful resource for my spiritual pilgrimage. Mine is marked and highlighted so I can find certain prayers easier. Across these years, I have participated in services and heard prayers that I did not know were in the prayer book. Sitting in Evensong—an afternoon service—in the marvelous Grace Cathedral in San Francisco, watching the sun's play on the stained-glass windows, I was moved when I heard one of the prayers and thanksgivings proclaiming God's truth in every age and by many voices.

Almighty God, you proclaim your truth in every age by many voices: Direct, in our time, we pray, those who speak where many listen and write what many read; that they may do their part in making the heart of this people wise, its mind sound, and its will righteous; to the honor of Jesus Christ our Lord. *Amen.*[68]

I had been troubled by the growing "hate talk" radio and the viciousness with which some Christians talk about our leaders. That prayer caught my attention because I am a writer and a speaker. When I called the cathedral and asked for a copy of the prayer, I was surprised to discover that it was from *The Book of Common Prayer*. I had missed it in my readings. There is always something fresh in the prayer book.

You should examine the following prayer books:

☐ *A Book of Prayers*, compiled by Ruth Connell (Lion), a small book I found in Canterbury Cathedral has been helpful as I travel. The prayers are grouped in themes with one prayer and a complementary quote on a page with lots of white space. That day in Canterbury, I found a little bookmarker that reminds me of the value of praying the prayers of others.

Almighty God, by your grace your martyrs shine as lights in the darkness of our times; grant that we may be so encouraged by their example and *strengthened by their prayers,* that we, too, may bear witness boldly to Christ, who is the light of life: through Jesus Christ, our Lord. Amen.[69]

What a great phrase, "strengthened by their prayers." For centuries, single adults have slipped into that great cathedral to pray; a few became martyrs. I need to be reminded of their lives and prayers. On days when I cannot compose my own prayers, I find strength in their prayers. Admittedly, a word or two strikes me as archaic, but never the thought behind the prayer.

"Thou who art over us, Thou who art one of us, Thou who art—Also within us, May all see thee—in me also, May I prepare the way for thee, May I thank thee for all that shall fall to my lot,—May I also not forget the needs of others, Keep me in thy love.—As thou wouldest that all should be kept in mine. May everything in this my being be directed to thy glory And may I never despair. For I am under thy hand, And in thee is all power and goodness." (Dag Hammarskjöld) [70]

"Give me a pure heart—that I may see thee, A humble heart—that I may hear thee, A heart of love—that I may serve thee, A heart of faith—that I may abide in thee." (Dag Hammarskjöld) [71]

"Lord, open our eyes to the world around us. Use us to warn people and tell them that when we walk hand in hand with you we are safe, even in the midst of a storm, and that there is an eternity to lose or gain." (Corrie ten Boom) [72]

"O Lord, calm the waves of this heart; calm its tempests. Calm thyself, O my soul, so that God is able to repose in thee, so that his peace may cover thee. Yes, Father in heaven, often have we found that the world cannot give us peace, Oh but make us feel that thou art able to give peace; let us know the truth of thy promise: that the whole world may not be able to take away thy peace." (Søren Kierkegaard) [73]

☐ *The Oxford Book of Prayer*, edited by George Appleton (Oxford University Press, 1985) includes prayers from across the long tradition of Christianity. Included are prayers of adoration, prayers from the Scripture, prayers of Christians, personal and occasional; prayers of the church; prayers as listening; prayers toward the unity of humankind. Reading through the name index is like a "who's who" of the faith.

This was prayed by a career bachelor Swedish diplomat, Secretary General of the United Nations, 1953–1961, who died in the secessionist Katanga province in what was then Belgian Congo trying to make peace. His classic spiritual journal, *Markings*, has touched thousands of lives.

Single parents or those who work with children will appreciate Marian Wright Edelman's *Guide My Feet: Prayers and Meditations on Loving and Working for Children* (Beacon, 1995) and Kerrie Hide's *A Woman's Healing Song: Prayers of Consolation for the Separated and Divorced* (Twenty-Third Publications, 1993).

Courteous God, sometimes I feel like such a failure;
I have so many regrets.
Help me to forgive myself,
    to forgive those who have hurt me, especially my
      partner.
Help me to experience your forgiveness.

Gentle one, loving one, it is time to make decisions,
    and yet I do not know what to do.
It's time to let go, to step out of the world I used to
    know.
What choices should I make?
Bless the decisions, O God; guide me in making
    them. [74]

African American readers and others will find *An African Prayer Book* (Doubleday, 1995) helpful. I keep my copy by my rocker. I find help in the black spirituals as well as some of the prayers from African tribes. As I read these my mind goes back to the scandalous (from the early Christian perspective) conversion of the Ethiopian eunuch, an African single adult who opened Africa to the gospel.

Lift Every Voice and Sing

God of our weary years, God of our silent tears,
Thou who has brought us thus far on the way;
Thou who hast by thy might led us into the
light; Keep us forever in the path, we pray.

Lest our feet stray from the places, our God,
where we met thee; Lest our hearts drunk with
the wine of the world, we forget thee; Shadowed
beneath thy hand, may we for ever stand,
True to our God, true to our native land. [75]

Many single adults have sung the song: "There is a balm in Gilead to make the wounded whole; There is a balm in Gilead to heal the sin-sick soul."

Sometimes I feel discouraged, And think my work's in vain,
But then the Holy Spirit revives my soul again.

If you can't preach like Peter, If you can't pray like Paul,
Just tell the love of Jesus, And say he died for all. [76]

☐ *Saint Benedict's Prayer Book* (Ampleforth Abbey Press, 1993) is a centuries-old text that has been chanted daily by the Benedictine monks. I have found, at the end of the day, when my will to pray is weak, I can turn to this book for a jump start, particularly in the prayers for each day of the week.

Visit, we pray you Lord, this house and this family, and drive far from it all the snares of the enemy. Let your holy angels dwell in this place for our protection and peace, and let your blessing be always upon us. Through Christ our Lord. Amen. May the Lord grant us (me) peace this night, and perfect peace hereafter. [77]

Take Lord, all my liberty, Receive my memory, my understanding, and my whole will. Whatever I have and possess, you have given me; to you I restore it wholly and to your will I utterly surrender it for my direction. Give me the love of you only, with your grace, and I am rich enough, I do not ask anything beside. Amen. [78]

Archbishop Desmond Tutu encourages us, "Let these prayers help you to become ever more and more fully what you already are: a child of God, known by name and whose very hairs are unnumbered. Praise and adore God and thank him for ever and ever." [79]

The key phrase in Tutu's admonition is, *"Let these prayers help you."* Recently, I had a rather painful reminder that it is one thing to pray another's prayers but another to practice the prayer: one thing to read the prayer but another to let the prayer read us, and become part of us. While writing this section, in the mornings I had been reading a little devotional book, *Forward Day by Day.* I was convicted by the prayer that is to be prayed daily for ninety days while reading that three-month devotional booklet:

I will try this day to live a simple, sincere and serene life, repelling every thought of discontent, anxiety . . . exercising economy in expenditure, generosity in giving, carefulness in conversation, diligence in appointed service, fidelity to every trust, and a childlike faith in God.[80]

I had been reading that prayer daily during the Christmas shopping season (or madness). Before I left to attend an Amish festival, I reminded myself of that phrase *"exercising economy in expenditure."* Unfortunately, I *read* rather than prayed it! Now, as I write this, days later, I am chagrined by what I spent that day on Christmas gifts! Fortunately, I did not charge any of it, but the Amish must have smiled when they saw me leaving. I had not allowed that prayer to settle down into my thinking so that I could live it out.

One of my favorite pray-ers is Thomas Merton. One opening sentence in a prayer of his is so helpful to me. "God, we have no idea where we are going. We do not see the road ahead of us."[81]

Take a moment and use these two sentences as your jump start. Run them through your imagination and compose your own prayer.

_____

_____

_____

As we approach the end of this section, I realize that some readers will have difficulty with this concept of "borrowing" the prayers of others. But if Jesus' dying prayer was not original, if he relied on the psalmist's prayer, "My God, my God, why have you forsaken me?"—it is okay for me to pray the prayers of others.

"We pray alone, of course, but we also pray as members of a community of faith, of a Church with a rich heritage and tradition. Our small prayers are inserted into the great stream of the Judeo-Christian liturgy, psalms, and devotions. These common prayers complement our personal petitions and raise worship above subjective expression." (Susan Muto) [82]

One last exercise may be of benefit to you. I have adapted it from C. S. Lewis's *The Screwtape Letters.*[83]

My Dear Wormwood:

It is about time that I write you about the subject of the spiritual life of (your name) _____. My best advice to you as for strategies that will be useful in keeping (your name) _____ from any serious or meaningful practice of prayer or the spiritual disciplines is:

Keep _____ busy with_____.

Keep _____ thinking about_____.

Remind _____ of_____.

Remind _____ that since God is_____.

And especially _____.

Take a moment and reflect on your responses. Ask God to dialogue with you concerning what you have written.

Prayer is God's invitation to dialogue!

You may not have chosen singleness. In fact, you may hate being single or single-again. Nevertheless, it is your reality at this point. Hammarskjöld bristled with his singleness, at times; yet, he could "take it to the Lord in prayer." Because he wrote his prayers in his journal, they can help me pray today.

"For all that has been—thanks! For all that shall be—yes!" (Dag Hammarskjöld) [84]

"Lord, it is enough that you alone see and know who I am and what I am doing. It is enough that you are aware of what my life as a single adult is all about." (Susan Muto) [85]

The only response to these two remarkable prayers is Amen!

Section 4

39. Journaling Your Fears ••••••••••••••••••••

Journaling is simple: write it down! See Section 1, Lesson 1 for a journal jump start.

"Then Samuel took a stone . . . named it Ebenezer, for he said, 'Thus far the LORD has helped us.'" —*1 Samuel 7:12*

"Pausing daily or a few times a week to jot down our thoughts has a way of quieting and uncluttering our overactive, decentered living. Writing helps us to work through detected obstacles to spiritual living. Words allow our real concerns to well up, enabling us to find back our lost center in Christ. A journal is not only a record of events that touch and transform us; it is a private space in which we can meet ourselves in relation to others and God." (Susan Muto) [1]

"I don't know who or what put the question. I don't know when it was put. I don't even remember answering. But at some moment I did answer Yes to Someone or Something—and from that hour I was certain that existence is meaningful and that, therefore, my life, in self-surrender, had a goal. And from that moment I have known what it means 'not to look back,' and 'to take no thought for the morrow.'" (Dag Hammarskjöld) [2]

How do you want to be remembered, especially if you do not have children? I want to be remembered as having tried to make a difference. During his life as a major player on the world diplomatic stage, Dag Hammarskjöld was a household name. This mover and shaper created the concept of "shuttle diplomacy" to diffuse world hot spots. However, he is not remembered primarily for his role as Secretary General of the United Nations, 1953–1961, or for having won the Nobel Peace Prize in 1961. Hammarskjöld is known for his spiritual journal, discovered after his death, and eventually published as *Markings*. This lifelong bachelor models the difference between being religious and being spiritual.

At the United Nations he had to be spiritually sensitive to the major world religions and the atheists who were part of the daily reality of his world. For the benefit of his own soul, he often slipped away to quiet New York City church sanctuaries and prayed for guidance. Outwardly, few labeled him religious.

I found *Markings* in a used books bookstore and paid less for an "unread" hardback than if I had bought it new in paperback. I have found great comfort in the musings and wisdom of a man who eventually gave his life as a peacemaker.

Define these two words:

Journal: _____

_____

Diary: _____

_____

Journaling is perhaps, in some sense, the simplest of the spiritual disciplines. However, it can be extremely difficult to stare at some of our soul's truth in black and white. Some of us are hamstrung by fear: fear that someone will "discover" our journal and sell its contents to *The National Enquirer* or *Hard Copy*. Well, someone could discover it—especially if we have roommates, are single parents and have children about, or if we are careless about where we put our journal(s). But, quite frankly, *The Enquirer* has bigger fish to fry.

> Take a moment and think about your experiences with writing about your life. What keeps you from journaling? What has kept you journaling?

I understand the fear, because I did not journal until it was a requirement in a seminary spirituality course I took. Then in doctoral work, journaling was a part of many of the classes. Of course, I had an option of folding over a page that I did not want the professor to read. We submitted our journals to be read for process, not content. But this was an opportunity to have experienced journalers help me journal more effectively and creatively. Otherwise, a journal is for your eyes only.

I remember one single parent protesting that she could not journal because of her eighteen-year-old daughter. "Why?" I pressed. "Oh, she snoops. She gets into my bedroom and goes through my things." I thought a moment and said, "You have a far more serious problem: a daughter who does not respect boundaries." But this was something of a convenient excuse for not journaling. Any excuse will do!

"Let's look at the deeper reason behind this objection. It is not so much a blockage due to grandiose fantasies as it may be an unwillingness to share ourselves even with ourselves, let alone with others and God. It takes courage to share at this level of reflection. It is understandable that we fear digging below the surface to disclose the deeper meanings of life." (Susan Muto) [3]

> What concerns or scares you about journaling?
>
> _____
> _____
> _____
> _____
> _____

For your protection, you might put a note on the cover of your journal: *This is a spiritual journal. Please respect my privacy and do not read it. If found, please return to . . .*

One of the big obstacles for many single adults is a tendency to self-edit. Or, to put ourselves in the best light, even to ourselves; this vulnerable writing might be read, perhaps, even after our death. One friend counters this notion: "What will it matter? You'll be dead!" If this is an issue, leave specific directions in your will and on the journals: Destroy.

On the other hand, the only thing I have received from a will is the journal of my friend Rusty. What a treasured experience to read his soul thoughts in his heroic struggles with dying. His incredible honesty about his life, his illness, his regrets.

Admittedly, my biggest fear is being real, being *completely* honest, even with myself. There are some things about myself that I do not want to know. Especially those that relate to sexual drives and desires, to ambitions, and ego. Years ago, when I was first divorced, late one night I painfully wrote these words:

> The tragedy of failure is to be able to see how close we were to success; that had we repeated our hope one more time, the temptation might have passed and in passing made us stronger for the future. I came so close to success and yet lost. And in losing, I found my weakness and confessed it.

Sharing those words leaves me open to readers pondering: "Ohhhh, wonder what that was about?" It was about my playing games with temptation and losing. I have carried that note with me for years as a reminder of the dangers of toying with temptation. A journal can be another type of reminder.

The other area where I have battled in my journal is with my unfulfilled ambition for a best-seller, for a book that would put me on every bookstore shelf in this country. I made the mistake of writing about this in *Forty Something and Still Single* and an angry reader wrote, "You big baby! What are you whining about? Some of us have never had our first book published!"

In journaling I have also written about my jealousy—and that is the right word—for the literary successes of some of my colleagues. Authors have a way of knowing how the books of others are doing. I have also "thrown in" the writer's towel a few times: "That's it! No more writing!" But just putting it on paper diffused some of the anger and woundedness.

In studying the spiritual disciplines I have been both helped and frustrated with suggestions from journaling teachers like Morton Kelsey, "Take an hour and write the ten deepest hungers of your heart."[4] I cannot easily do that because it would put my heart under a microscope and I prefer to pretend that I am so spiritual. My friend Dr. Frank Freed asks counselees, "What are you pretending not to know?" The journal asks, "What are you pretending not to know *about yourself?*"

Maybe I need to have a T-shirt made that says:

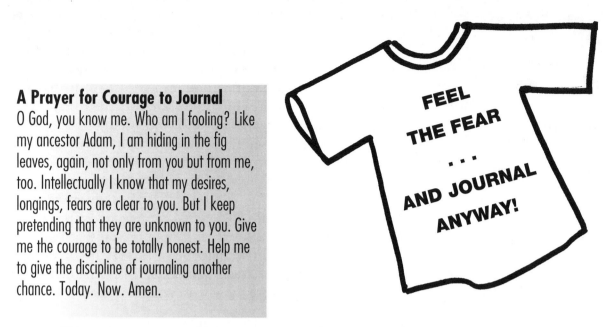

FEEL THE FEAR . . . AND JOURNAL ANYWAY!

40. The Nuts and Bolts of Journaling • • • • • • • • • • • • •

You don't have to "do" journaling perfectly. All you need is a piece of paper, a pencil or pen, and a willingness to write the first word of the first sentence.

"We spend our years as a tale that is told."
—*Psalm 90:9 KJV*

My doctoral research was in the area of storytelling. I believe all of us are storytellers and the most important story is the story we know the best: our own. Morton Kelsey says that some of us do not value ourselves enough to reflect seriously on our lives. "I am in a certain sense cheating both God and the world when I do not make a reflective, imaginative record of my inner being. I have a place, a value, and a destiny which no other person can fulfill."[5]

> Our losses do not change; what changes are the stories we make out of those losses.

Take a moment and reread Kelsey's words. How do you respond to them?

I have long been struck by the words I read on the grave of Lee Atwater, once head of the Republican National Party and White House adviser, "I do not choose to be a common man, it is my God-given right to be uncommon." Journaling is a record of our uncommonness, or our struggle to be uncommon. And journals remind us of an outrageous, accompanying God who is with us on our pilgrimages. The God who dusts us off and says, "Come on" or "Up you go!" The God who dares to let us catch glimpses of him.

This is especially important for single adults who have experienced the "black-and-blues" of singleness. These wounds become raw resources for spiritual growth. Frederick Buechner reminds us:

> Maybe nothing is more important than that we keep track, you and I, of these stories of who we are and where we have come from and the people we have met along the way because it is precisely through these stories in all their particularity. . . That God makes himself known to each of us more powerfully and personally. If this is true, it means that to lose track of our stories is to be spiritually impoverished not only humanly but also spiritually.[6]

Why should a single adult journal?

> Place a check in the boxes that represent your experiences and desires. Then a star by the one most true for you.

"I thought it highly expedient, for my own satisfaction and the confirmation of my friends, to keep an impartial diary of my intentions, resolutions, and actions, as a Christian and a minister, that I might have, through this medium, a constant and reasonable answer for my accusers." (Francis Asbury)[7]

☐ To grow in self-understanding
☐ To aid our devotional lives
☐ For guidance and decision making
☐ To make sense and order of our lives
☐ To release emotions and gain perspective
☐ To have greater awareness of daily life
☐ For self-expression and creativity
☐ To clarify beliefs
☐ To set goals
☐ To work through problems

Kathryn Kolb, an American single adult held hostage in Iran for over a year, journaled on the backs of envelopes: "My journal helped me remember my reactions and some things I had read. It also reminded me of things I wanted to think about more deeply and help crystallize my thinking."[8]

"When I look through the contents of previous journal entries, I can see the album of my life's journey during the past four years. There are days when I scaled the mountain top of joy, and there are other times when I slogged through the grimy valley of discouragement. But I can see that God has been both places with me." (Nathan Harms)[9]

One of my friends was so concerned that I, as a writer, did not journal, that he bought me an expensive leather journal for Christmas. "There! Now there's no reason not to journal." Unfortunately, that journal became the reason *not* to write: what thoughts of mine are that worthy? I ended up buying several blank journal books in a bookstore but I did not write in these because I may make a mistake or get too vulnerable. Finally, I started journaling in a dime store-variety spiral notebook. I found a great deal of freedom because if I made a mistake I could simply rip it out, crumple the page, and "shoot" toward the nearest wastebasket. Now I do most of my journaling on my laptop. That leather journal still waits for me.

Ron Klug, whose *How to Keep a Spiritual Journal* has helped many novice journalists and insists that there are no rules. "Your way of keeping a journal is the right way."[10] Of course, helpful hints can be gained from veteran journalers.

You can keep momentum in journaling by:

☐ Being honest: write how you really feel not how you think you should feel.

☐ Getting at the gut feeling level. Why play it safe in your journal? Use the exact word you feel, not a polite synonym. The psalmists did not self-edit their emotions.

☐ Experimenting with your journal. It's yours. Be creative. Richard Foster, who authored *Celebration of Discipline*, draws and sketches in his journal. Feel free to glue or tape in pictures. Use different colors of ink.

☐ Not taking journaling too seriously. Don't turn this into another chore to be checked-off.

☐ Inserting quotations for future reference. These can become jump starters for moments you are stuck. Some of the quotes by single adults in the left columns of this book may prove helpful starters.

 When you find yourself "tongue tied" or with journaler's block, try to begin your journal entry like a letter to a friend:

Dear _____ . . .

It may sound silly, but people have used this method for centuries. If you have a trusted friend with whom you share some of your heart's secrets, why not pretend you are writing a letter to him or her? Of course, you can always address your entry to the most trusted Friend of all, God.[11]

Use a computer. More and more of my journaling is done on my laptop. I have found that the fonts and sizing make my journal more creative. I have a feeling—journal purists may disagree—that the "great" journalers, John Wesley, David Brainerd, Thomas Merton, Francis Asbury, would use laptops if they were with us today. This also adds an element of security to my journal.

But there are still times I want the "feel" of an ink pen on paper. Give yourself permission to journal *your* way.

You shall not mimic another's journal style!

"My journal is a special treat I allow myself, a personal and limitless means of expression." (Nathan Harms) [12]

A journal offers a safe place to interact with the romantic wounds and bruises of the heart. A journal offers us a place to bear the black-and-blue wounds of dating, of relationships that don't make it to the finish line, misunderstandings, the painful realization that you are not "enough"—that hope-tainting moment when you realize that this relationship is en route to the romantic junk heap.

Nathan Harms illustrates this point with a journal letter he wrote after hours of tossing and turning:

Dear Rebecca: I know you will never read this letter, but here are some things I need to tell you or I simply won't be able to sleep tonight . . .

I wrote all the things I could never have said to Rebecca, things I really wouldn't want to say to her verbally. I stopped at the end of several pages to read what I had written. I knew the words didn't express the objective truth of my situation, but they did express *my* feelings at the moment. I knew I would never give her the letter; I also knew I didn't need to.[13]

Journals are a safe place to tidy up the romantic clutter of our lives.

Journals are a safe place to grapple with our romantic regrets.

Reviewing journals may help us place a particular romantic loss into perspective.

Journaling Our Good-byes

Most single adults have to eventually say good-bye to relationships, friendships, work relationships; sometimes, it's to fantasies, dreams, hopes. Some of us have been through the "great" good-bye when a spouse died or when we went through divorce. We have been devastated when the relationship we thought would make it to the finish line ended. Sometimes there are things we later wish we had said. Sometimes, parting words didn't come out as we hoped. I believe we can do anticipatory good-byes through our journals or finalize our good-byes there.

Some components in a healthy good-bye letter from Benjamin Cirlin, a New York City grief counselor, might be valuable:
- [ ] *When I think of saying good-bye, I feel . . .*
- [ ] *I remember when we . . .*
- [ ] *The most important element of our relationship, to me, has been . . .*
- [ ] *When we are no longer together, I will miss . . .*
- [ ] *The thing I most regret about saying good-bye is . . .*
- [ ] *When I think of a future without you, I feel . . .*[14]

This exercise will be more helpful if you invite God to be with you in this journal experience. After you have a good draft, pause to pray, "God, the One who knows me best, have I left out something?" Have I been honest?

What do you do with the "good-bye" letter? You could:
- [ ] Burn it.
- [ ] Mail it to yourself and re-read it at a later date.
- [ ] Do nothing with the letter.

I would not recommend mailing the letter to the individual. This good-bye letter is in the context of your journaling, for your benefit.

You might want to take a look at the good-byes that the apostle Paul wrote.

The Broadway show tune, "I'm Going to Wash That Man Right Out of My Hair" could be amended, "I'm Going to Journal That Man/Woman Right Out of My Heart. . . ."

Name some people that you need to write a good-bye letter to.

1. _____

2. _____

3. _____

Journal and diary are not synonyms. A diary records the events of the day "events and occurrences." A journal, however, is about the implications of those events. Ben Campbell Johnson observed, "A journal takes what is recorded and puts it into a larger context or imbues it with a deeper meaning."[15]

A diary answers the question: "What happened today?" The journal answers the question: "Now what?" or "So what?"

The diary says, "This happened." The journal says, "This is *why* I think it happened."

You may need some breaks from journaling. If you are facing circumstances that you do not want to be honest about, it is easier to play pretend. Or your schedule can be so heavy and you do not have time to write long entries. The alternative is to write for five minutes. Klug says there are times we "choose to take a vacation from your journal,"[16] or give yourself permission not to journal. I confess that while writing this book, because I was behind schedule, I did not journal as faithfully as I wished. However, I found some of the writing of this material reminds of what I have discovered about journaling.

After her father's death, one of my single friends discovered that he had "journaled" in his Bible. He had long been concerned because she had not married. One day, while casually skimming it she found a note beside a heavily underlined verse, "This day I have peace about my Becky." To this day, she treasures the verse and the notation. A journal can be your place to voice hopes, fears, frustrations.

It is also important to re-read journals.

"Re-reading old journals convinces us that our life was not haphazard." (Susan Muto)[17]

"Immense mountains are relativized into normal molehills, once I see them sketched on paper." (Susan Muto)[18]

"Through the medium of my journal, I can look back upon what God hath wrought, and say, 'Hitherto the Lord hath helped.' We can thus comfort and console ourselves with the past lovingkindness of the Lord; and the years in which his right hand hath been bare, will thus, to us, be rendered more delightful." (Francis Asbury)[19]

Sometimes, we need signposts in the midst of a storm, where we can go back and see other "storms" we have weathered, other crises: so that we can be reminded that the God who was so faithful in that situation will be faithful in the current ones and in those yet to come.

For further reading:

Adams, Kathleen, *Journal to the Self* (New York: Warner, 1990).

Kelsey, Morton T., *Adventure Inward: Christian Growth Through Personal Journal Writing* (Minneapolis: Augsburg, 1980).

Klug, Ronald, *How to Keep a Spiritual Journal* (Minneapolis: Augsburg, 1994).

41. Keeping a Lookout for God • • • • • • • • • • • • • • • • •

It's this simple: Pay Attention

"When I look at your heavens, the work of your fingers . . . what are human beings that you are mindful of them?" —*Psalm 8:3-4*

"There are times when each of us feels under siege, bombarded by powerful resources which seem to be destroying our very tranquility. In just such times we are called to have an eye out for the signs of the love of God."[20]

Those words leaped out at me one morning during my devotional reading. Yes, I do read daily devotional books but as *one* ingredient, not *the* ingredient in my devotional life. I was amazed by how this quote tied to something about George Washington Carver I had read an hour earlier—especially in light of the fact that this morning I was scheduled to write on "noticing." Some single adults would say it's a coincidence, but I see providence. Providence often comes in "interruptible" moments, when I collide with the reality of God in the world. Some of my most incredible devotional moments were not "scheduled" in the Daytimer. It can be as simple as looking up, looking around, noticing, staying aware of our surroundings and not giving in to the subtle temptation to "numb out."

"As I sat in my little 'den' reading and pondering over it, nature came to my relief when I was attracted by a strangely mellow light falling upon the paper. I looked up and out the window toward the setting sun, which was just disappearing behind the horizon leaving a halo of never-to-be forgotten glory and beauty behind it. It seems as if I have never been conscious of such beauty and sublimity. The variety, brilliancy of color and arrangement were awe inspiring. As I came to myself I said aloud, O God, I thank Thee for such a direct manifestation of Thy goodness, majesty and power." (George Washington Carver) [21]

How can you keep "an eye out for the signs of the love of God"?

By _____

_____

By _____

_____

By _____

_____

I had an encounter with God and a spectacular sunset the Sunday after Thanksgiving 1995. I was driving east on I-70 to St. Louis—two hours behind schedule—when I happened to look in the rearview mirror and saw the sunset. I even turned around in the seat to see it. For the next several minutes I kept turning around. Finally, I pulled off I-70 and sat in a field watching God at the control board of the Missouri sky. Most nights angels are in charge of sunsets, but that night I saw God's signature across the heavens in oranges and pinks and scarlets. I savored the experience of noticing, even though I had to remind myself that noticing the sunset was time well spent.

God goes to so much effort to create beauty and we take it for granted. Such moments offer me a generous insight into the God who loves me.

I was reminded that all of us can make time when I read this anecdote about Martha Berry, founder of Berry College in Georgia. She had stooped down, wrote one friend, to cup a large pink tulip in both hands, softly saying, "Oh, if only in my short life I could praise God so exquisitely as you do."[22]

"Frequently, as one drives around the country roads of Bond County—as I like to do, especially when goldenrod and black-eyed susans and ironweed are on winding roadsides with yellows and purples—as one drives toward Hillsboro or Centralia or Carlisle or Carbondale . . . Alert eyes can see them often: the solitary trees, on hill crests or in field edges. . . . emanating a sense of self-respect, ease, power, poise, grace. Gloriously proportioned symmetry. Ever since I moved to southern Illinois, the splendid solitary trees have seemed to me to present an interesting analogy with what can happen to a personality, alone, and with room to grow."
(Elva McAllaster)[23]

When was the last time you stopped to watch nature unfold?

Date:

_____

Location: _____

What I saw: _____

To celebrate the experience I . . .

☐ prayed

☐ sang

☐ invited someone, "Come look at this . . ."

☐ told someone about it

☐ journaled about it

☐ pretty much forgot about it until just now.

One consequence of our urbanized life is that we don't have time to stop and notice the roses. A widow came up and cried, "My husband never took time to smell the roses!" I responded, "What was so unusual about that?" She answered, "He was a florist." As Christians, should we be about the business of noticing, enjoying, and commenting on our Creator's handiwork?

We have all seen solitary trees. A single adult named Elva saw an analogy to her own life. She noticed and journaled. We need such time-outs from the stress: to ponder, to gaze, to be reminded of things as simple as solitary trees in the middle of pastures. That's why I made time in the Christmas season to wander through the poinsettia exhibit arranged by the Kansas City Parks Board. I saw twelve varieties such as celebrate, angelika-pink, pink peppermint, jingle bells, marble, lemon drop, and the Japanese supjibi. I could have dashed in, done a quick walk through: been there, done that. What's next on the Christmas to-do list? But I spent time really noticing these gorgeous plants and being reminded that God likes diversity.

When I was going through divorce in North Carolina—big-time broke—many nights I sat on my porch in the mountain night air and admired the spectacular creativity of God. More than one sleepless night, I pulled a blanket and went out on the lawn for a stretched-out view. Now I have to make time for such encounters, but those are the "feeding times" for my soul.

My friend Dr. Steve Bearden, a single adult minister in Salem, Oregon, initially annoyed me with his musings on the stars in his monthly newsletter. But I have come to hear the question asked of the disciples after the Ascension, "Why do you stand looking up toward heaven?" (Acts 1:11). A good answer is, *because it is there*. Or, as one single adult told me, "Because my Father made them. They offer clues as to what he is like." Now, I have gone a step farther and installed light-absorbing stars in the ceiling of my bedroom. All day long they collect light; then at night, I sleep "under the stars."

"I want them to see the Great Creator in the smallest and apparently the most insignificant things about them." (George Washington Carver) [24]

God has filled this universe with amazing things to notice. Just consider the mind-boggling discoveries of the Hubble Telescope. Even scientists stare in amazement! In an agrarian age, people had to read the skies for approaching weather changes; now we flip on the Weather Channel. The poets have had richly wonderful vocabularies to identify snowfalls and thunderstorms. Many of us settle for the plainest of adjectives: *pretty* or *beautiful*. Sadly, our noticing skills are pretty underdeveloped.

Vacations offer us a change of scenery and an opportunity to store up memories for future replay. The most unusual vacation of my life was during the writing of this book when I got to spend two weeks in Hawaii. My photos did not capture the splendor and beauty. Vacations can be a chance to see, close-up, God's craftmanship, such as the night skies of Hawaii. I did not have sufficient vocabulary to capture what I saw.

For some single adult friends, it has been ski country that has offered their speechless encounter with God the Creator; or the picturesque Sadona Mountains in Arizona; or the stillness of Cade's Cove in the Smokies.

The objective is not just being a tourist in those settings, but being a spiritual pilgrim as well while your camera becomes your journal.

"Just last week I was reminded of His omnipotence, majesty and power through a little specimen of mineral sent me for analysis, from Bakersfield, California. I dissolved it, purified it, made conditions favorable for the formation of crystals, when lo before my very eyes, a beautiful bunch of sea green crystals have formed and alongside them a bunch of snow white ones. Marvel of marvels, how I wish I had you in God's little workshop for a while, how your soul would be thrilled and lifted up." (George Washington Carver) [25]

Where are your "little workshop" places or your favorite "time-out" spots, that nurture your soul?

_____
_____
_____
_____

And other people's postcards—those "Having a great time—wish you were here" cards can also be useful for journals or "jump starters." For example, I had always said I would never go to Hawaii as a single adult because it was "too romantic." Well, nearly fifty years old, I finally decided to get over that nonthinking—but a couple of postcards from friends did nudge me on.

I also keep postcards and use them for bookmarks. Sometimes those postcard bookmarks have reminded me to pray for the friend who sent the card. God has gone to great trouble to make so many beautiful spots in the world. Don't let being single keep you from experiencing as many of them as possible.

42. $ingle $ensibility •

"Stingy Christian" is an oxymoron.

"Make every effort to send Zenas the lawyer and Apollos on their way, and see that they lack nothing." —*Titus 3:13*

"I have the assurance that God will take care of me. He blessed me with the ability to earn a living, and gives me wisdom and understanding enough to lay a little by from time to time for the proverbial 'rainy day.'" (George Washington Carver) [26]

I doubt that Paul's advice to Titus is the favorite to many single adults. Especially if you ponder its tag-team verse in 2 Corinthians 8:15, which basically says that your plenty will supply their need. *My* plenty? Have you seen my checkbook? I cannot remember the last time I had some "plenty" to give away. Unfortunately, most single adults compare themselves to wealthy people like Ross Perot or Steve Forbes or Warren Buffet or Bill Gates, and think that verse is designed for the rich. Sorry—but it is for all of us. Trips to China and to Haiti forever changed my understanding of wealth. By the standards of Christian single adults in those two countries, I am wealthy. The monthly per capita income in China is what I spend on Diet

Coke or at McDonald's in a month. I am reminded that many of the things I consider necessities (hot running water, for example) are luxuries in those two cultures.

Be generous and willing to share.
(See 1 Timothy 6:18.)

Perhaps the real test of spirituality is not looking through a single adult's Bible but rather through his or her checkbook. How do you spend "your" money?

Name your five top financial priorities each month.

1. _____
2. _____
3. _____
4. _____
5. _____

"We are rarely willing to examine closely the role that financial security plays in our lives. It is insidious because it has wormed its way into our lives so subtly and so completely that we really believe having money means being in paradise. It is often the last corner of our lives that we are willing to let go of." (Bill Huebsch) [27]

"When you have eaten your fill and have built fine houses and live in them, and when your herds and flocks have multiplied, and your silver and gold is multiplied, and all that you have is multiplied, then do not exalt yourself, forgetting the LORD your God, who brought you out of the land of Egypt, out of the house of slavery."—*Deuteronomy 8:12-14*

"Do not say to yourself, 'My power and the might of my own hand have gotten me this wealth.' But remember the LORD your God, for it is he who gives you power to get wealth."
—*Deuteronomy 8:17-18*

Giving is an opportunity to invest in causes, organizations, institutions that will exist long after we have passed from this scene. By giving, we can participate in answering someone's prayer.

Moses warned the Israelites that it would be easy to "forget" to praise the Lord, and they needed to commit themselves to obedience.

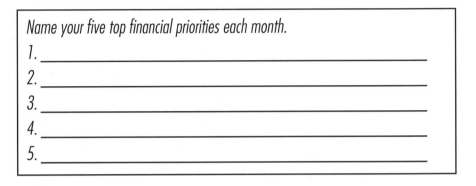

Take a moment and slowly reread Moses' words, translating "herds and flocks" into your profession. For example: When you buy a fine condo and hire an interior decorator, when your investments prosper, and your car is fast and sleek . . .

_____

_____

_____

Moses' warning is a stinging reminder to single adults whose credit cards are topped out, whose closets are full, and whose desires for "bigger, better, and more" are being fanned by advertising.

Deuteronomy 8: 17-18 is on my financial journal, where I keep track of my expenses and inside my checkbook cover so that I can be reminded. Each paycheck is an opportunity for a

"Thank-you." A particular employer is my resource; God is my source. It is tempting to get that backward.

 You may want to go back and read all of Deuteronomy chapter eight, but focus on verses 17 and 18. What does God want to say to you?

Take a moment and use this verse, form a prayer: God, I acknowledge that you have given me the ability to produce wealth although I don't think my income qualifies as wealth. Remind me. . .

43. Giving Ourselves

It is easier to reach for my checkbook or wallet than for my Daytimer.
"And let people learn to devote themselves to good works in order to meet urgent needs."
—Titus 3:14

I served for a number of years on the Board of Trustees of Scarritt College in Nashville. I often felt frustrated by my inability to give large amounts of money to the school. Some trustees earned monthly, weekly, what I made in a year. But the experience did teach me something about giving what I could. As well as "stretch" giving and trusting God to supply the difference, for example, a tax refund larger than I had anticipated, I learned that some trustees give money, others give wisdom, and some service.

"I have learned in my years on earth to hold everything loosely, because when I hold them tightly, God has to pry my fingers away, and that hurts." (Corrie ten Boom) [28]

"If I can stop one heart from breaking I shall not live in vain. If I can ease one life the aching or cool one pain; Or help one fainting robin unto his nest again, I shall not live in vain."
(Emily Dickinson) [29]

Two simple words of advice: *Get involved.* All around us are causes, issues, organizations that need our time and talent as well as our financial resources, either as volunteers or in board leadership.

"I craved . . . for something worth doing instead of frittering time away on useless trifles." (Florence Nightingale) [30]

"O God, since you have enabled me to do the simple things that I can do, I have full trust in You to do the great things which I cannot."
(Lillian Thrasher) [31]

God does not ask about our *ability* but rather about our *avail*-ability. Volunteering and service are ways to use our time and talents, often in ways that will live long after we have gone.

> "He who serves God with what costs him nothing, will do very little service, you may depend on it." (Susan Warner) [32]

Emily might have passed unknown through life; tuberculosis might have remained a great medical killer in this country. Might have. But this Sunday school teacher chose to "do something" about the then-dreaded killer. In 1907, she set up a booth in the Wilmington, Delaware post office selling stamps to put on Christmas cards. On the seals was a red cross. A tradition was born! Christmas seals have raised millions to support research and service through the American Lung Association. It began with a single adult, Emily Bissell, who spent forty years of her life as a volunteer. [34]

It's tempting to ask, "What can I do? I am *only* a single adult!" Well, spend some time exploring the lives of single adults like Mabel Broadman (Red Cross), Clara Barton (Red Cross), or the single adults who have been quoted in the left-hand margins of this book, and you will discover how volunteers have left this cultural landscape forever changed.

> "Service is the price you pay for your space you occupy." (Eartha M. M. White) [33]
>
> "In a world where there is so much to be done, I felt strongly impressed that there must be something for me to do." (Dorothea Dix) [35]

I have been taken by the quotation that I am told is on the mirror of the Jesuit writer John Powell, "Hey, God, what have you got going on today? I'd like to be part of it." [36] What would happen if you put those words on your bathroom mirror and read them for the next thirty days?

> I dare you to put Powell's words in a place where you will notice them daily.
>
> "Do all the good you can for all the people you can." (Eartha M. M. White) [37]

> Take a moment and reread the Dix and Powell quotations in notes 35 and 36 respectively. Think about volunteer opportunities in your area. Have you said, "If I had the time, I would like to . . ."? How could you go about exploring volunteer opportunities? How can you go about asking, "Hey, God, what have you got going on in my community that I could be part of?"
>
> I could _____.
>
> I could _____.

> "We should always look upon ourselves as God's servants, placed in God's world, to do his work; and accordingly labour faithfully for him; . . . to glorify God, and to do all the good we possibly can." (David Brainerd) [38]

The next time you encounter a request for volunteers, prayerfully consider that this could be an opportunity for servanthood with your name monogrammed on it.

I like what orator Edward Everett Hale wrote to single adult Helen Keller:

I AM ONLY ONE, but still I am one. I cannot do everything, but I can do something; And because I cannot do everything I will not refuse to do the something that I can do.[39]

Always be able to look back and say, "At least I didn't live no humdrum life!" (Forest Gump) [40]

Volunteering is a marvelous way to avoid the humdrum life that is such a seduction in our society. Get involved.

"You never become truly spiritual by sitting down and wishing to become so. You must undertake something so great that you cannot accomplish it unaided. Begin doing something for your fellowmen and if you do it with all your power, it will almost immediately bring you face to face with problems you cannot solve; you need God and you need to go to God." (Phillips Brooks) [41]

"You don't know what you can do, until you try! God never puts anyone in a place too small to grow in!" (Henrietta Mears) [42]

44. Making Silence ●

God rarely yells to get a single adult's attention.

"Be still before the LORD." —Psalm 37:7

Racket. Noise. Where can I go to find silence? How can I make silence? Even the people with headphones play their walkmans at such a high level that the fine whine intrudes into my silent places.

I remember standing with a friend in the great Trinity Church in Boston, a sense of awe enfolding me. There was sheer silence after the noise of the busy Boston streets. My friend leaned over and said, "Wouldn't you love to hear (and he named a major Christian musical group) perform in here?"

"No!" I thought. "What could be better than this particular silence?"

Many single adults have great difficulty with silence. "Don't just sit there. Say something!" which almost means, "Say anything." Silence makes us uncomfortable. We turn to televisions, radios, CD players, and noisemakers. Many of us do not even sleep in silence. Radios are our night-lights—our equivalents of Linus's blanket. How do we *make* silence?

> "Oh, how we need the quiet times to let God speak to us." (Belle Bennett) [43]

> "The temple of our purest thoughts is silence!" (Sarah J. Hale) [44]

> "We live in silence except when we fill it with noise." (Bill Huebsch) [45]

> "Everything has its wonders, even darkness and silence, and I learn, whatever state I may be in, therein to be content." (Helen Keller) [46]

> "Steal away to a quiet place." (Eartha M. M. White) [47]

☐ *Turn off the radio, television, noisemakers.* If this is difficult, set aside silence zones or time outs from deliberate noise. Thirty minutes or an hour of silence, although initially difficult, can become a welcome relief from all the noise clutter of our day.

☐ *Drive or commute in silence.* I remember once driving 500 miles without listening to the radio. I arrived at my destination relaxed.

☐ *Find places of silence.* It used to be the library, but that mandate of silence is the exception and is going by the wayside. During the week church sanctuaries offer silent spaces—if you can find one that is open. Fortunately, many Catholic and Episcopal churches are open during the day.

☐ *Find natural sanctuaries.* Several years ago I found Cades' Cove in the Great Smoky Mountains National Park. Ironically, you find zillions of tourists and shoppers in the outlet malls and shops of Pigeon Forge and downtown Gatlinburg, but if you make your way to Cades' Cove, you can park your car, walk a few hundred yards and suddenly be esconced in silence. On a fall afternoon it can be ecstasy!

☐ *Ask people to turn down the volume.* I cannot understand why people drag boom boxes to pools and the beach. What good is the sun without the sound of the surf? When someone shows up with an industrial size boom box, I want to paraphrase Little Red Riding Hood, "My! What a big boom box you have." I used to think someone would kick sand in my face, but now I politely ask, "Would you *mind* [or please] turning down the music!" I have also asked waiters or hostesses, "Does the music have to be *that* loud?" in restaurants.

☐ *Open yourself to God.* Thomas Keating reminds us that God can speak to us "not only with words but also with the secret inspirations of grace."[48] We don't have to ask, "Who's there?" We can learn to recognize the sound of God's presence.

Admittedly it would be easier if we wore plastic signs, "Do Not Disturb." But sometimes we have to create and then maintain the silence. This is one luxury of the single life.

I remember spending a week at Bon Secours Convent in Maryland. Every afternoon during the three-day silence, many participants in the spirituality seminar gathered and rocked in large comfortable rockers. Sitting in a large circle for an hour, in an experience the nuns called "shared presence," we enjoyed the shared silence. It was a remarkable experience, although I must admit that eating in silence was difficult.

☐ *Consider silence a "fasting" from noise.* Some of us justify the noise in our world because we listen to "Christian" music or to "good" music or "mellow" music. Noise is still noise and is an intrusion into the space of the soul. Our electricity-generated world means a constant sound of motors and rhythms (clocks, lawn mowers, household machines, and so forth). Our ears hardly hear them anymore, but our souls do. Hear the psalmist's admonition, "Be still before the LORD" (37:7).

Stop reading for a moment. Listen. Identify the sounds you hear:

I hear _____ , which is _____.
I hear _____ , which is _____.
I hear _____ , which is _____.

In the space in the right-hand column, quantify that sound: pleasurable, unpleasant, or distracting. Now spend a moment asking: Why is that sound there?

Every maturing believer needs time of silence, creative silence, silence to hear the still small voice of God, a God who does not yell over the distracting noises in our culture, much of which has to do with buying, consuming, using, acquiring. God longs for us to experience in silence what Thomas Keating calls "at-easeness," which he compares to the elderly pair "who don't have to talk all the time but sometimes like to sit and watch the sunset together."[49]

How do you deliberately make silence in your life?

1. _____
2. _____
3. _____

Go through your home or apartment and identify the ongoing sources of noise. Then identify the occasional sources of noise.

I was surprised by an ad in a flight magazine that read, "In a world of pagers, faxes, and cellular phones, sometimes you just need to get in touch with yourself." The ad was not for religious-based materials or for a monastery offering overnight accommodations for spiritual pilgrims, but for a portable spa. The company even called its product "a sanctuary."

Speak, Lord, *this* single adult is listening. Lord, teach me to be comfortable with the silence of my life. Teach me to invite you to join me in my silence.

☐ *Invite God to accompany you into the silence and to speak.* In the Old Testament, young Samuel whispered into the night, "Speak, for your servant is listening" (1 Samuel 3:10). Those words are still appropriate. In the silence try using Samuel's invitation.

My mother often told me that as a widow, she turned the television on "for company." "It gets so lonely at night, with no one to talk to." Those lonely moments can be incredible opportunities to say, "Speak, Lord, for your servant is listening." But also remember the Scripture repeatedly telling us that Jesus sought out the lonely places to pray.

"It seems to have been in the silence of his life that Jesus heard God's voice most clearly. In the quiet of the desert, pondering his own calling, sorting through the events of life up to that point, he learned what it means to be a child of God." (Bill Huebsch) [50]

We too need a decent place—a quiet place.

The world invites us to flee from the silence. God invites us to flee into the silence and to befriend the silence.

I suspect not only the lonely places but also the lonely times Jesus turned into times to pray.

> So when you're lonely where do you go? What do you do?
>
> _____ eat   _____ do housework
> _____ shop   _____ do my nails
> _____ exercise   _____ go for a drive
>
> or _____

45. Changing the *Core Un'Grato* • • • • • • • • • • • • • • •

"Thank you" is a vital ingredient in a devotional life.

". . . giving thanks to God the Father at all times and for everything in the name of our Lord Jesus Christ."—*Ephesians 5:20*

"Thank you, O Lord, for another day to work." (Martha Berry) [51]

Too many single adults possess a *core un'grato*, an ungrateful heart. Their attitude on gratitude focuses on a bare ring finger. That really snuffs out even the seedlings of gratitude. Giving thanks to God "for everything" definitely does not include singleness.

My friend Elva McAllaster proposed a Doxology Day for single adults. We honor birthdays and anniversaries so why not a day to celebrate our singleness?

"I hate being single!" "I don't want to draw attention to my singleness." "I'm not about to throw a hypocritical party to celebrate what I hate, nor to praise God for being single." These are some of the objections to Dr. Elva McAllaster's idea. She still reminds us, "the Christian way of life is to praise God in all things."[52]

"... singing and making melody to the Lord in your hearts, giving thanks to God the Father at all times and for everything in the name of our Lord Jesus Christ." —*Ephesians 5:19, 20*

Dr. McAllaster's idea does have a "biblical" ring to it. After all, Paul—who had been beaten, jailed, whipped, shipwrecked, bitten by a snake, and ultimately lost his head—encourages us to celebrate our thankfulness. This is a single adult talking to us!

Dr. McAllaster's "Doxology Day" is an easy day to calculate. It is six months from your birthday. My birthday is August 21; so my Doxology Day would be February 21. On that day I could:

☐ Change my image for the day.

☐ Dust off an activity that I have previously enjoyed but haven't had time for in my normal routine.

☐ Send myself a card or a singing telegram.

☐ Take the day off.

☐ Do something so totally outrageous that it will leave my friends befuddled!

☐ Do something for someone else.

But I have found that the best way to change a *core un'grato* is by getting in the habit of saying lots of "thank-you's" first to my Creator for the gift of life and then to my fellow residents on planet Earth.

Set aside some time for reflection: To whom am I grateful? I have some friends who send "thank-you" cards to their parents on their own birthdays thanking their parents for bringing them into this world. It's never too late to say "thank you." Someone could get a big blessing from a "thank-you" card or note today.

A Thanksgiving Prayer

So often I hear word of thanks for good things You have done,

An answered prayer, a miracle, a day with only sun.

But I am here to offer thanks for gifts sent in disguise,
The things You use at other times despite my groans and sighs.

For I have seen Your hand of good can come in many forms,

And often in my life the growth has come
because of storms.

The painful loss, the dream denied, the trial and
the woe,
Have been the means, so often Lord, Your
faithfulness to show.

Protection sure and guidance clear in retrospect
I see,
And in the very things I shunned You showed
Yourself to me.

So at this time of giving thanks my thanks is
something new;
I thank You, Lord, for thorny paths, that led me
close to You.[53]

A Prayer to Become More Thankful

*Where do I begin to give thanks to you? I feel so ungrateful.
Gratitude has not been my strong suit. But this day I pause
deliberately to say "Thank you" for all your many benefits,
many of which I do not fully comprehend. Thank you, Father, for*

_____

_____

_____

*I would like to propose a little spiritual exercise that I
enjoy, particularly on Thanksgiving Day, my birthday, or
New Year's Day.*
- [ ] *Make some quiet time and space.*
- [ ] *Read Psalm 139.*
- [ ] *Recite the prayer in the left margin and add, "Bring to my
  mind that for which I need to offer thanks especially for . . ."*
- [ ] *In the space below begin listing the things for which you
  are grateful:*

_____   _____

_____   _____

_____   _____

_____   _____

*Set aside a page in your journal. At the top of the page write,
"I am grateful . . ."*

It very ill becomes a creature to partake of
benefits from his God, and then to forget his
heavenly benefactor. . . . The matter of our
thanksgivings may be arranged under these
two heads: we must give thanks for those
benefits for which we have prayed, and for
those which God has conferred upon us without
praying for.[54]

Take a moment to list items in Watts's two categories:

Benefits I have prayed for	*Benefits I have not prayed for*
_____	_____
_____	_____
_____	_____

1. Here are some primers to get the gratitude flowing:

   - People who have made a difference in my life
   - Friends
   - Professional achievements or milestones
   - Places I have visited
   - Wonderful moments
   - Realities such as good health, your relationship with God

2. Then read your list aloud, frequently saying, "I am grateful for . . ."
3. Date the list for future reference. Then, take one page and draw a line down the center. On the left side write "Things I am not thankful for . . ." On the other side write, "Things I am unsure about . . ." Literally, for some items, the jury is still out; but time converts what we thought was a curse into a blessing.

Be prepared to spend some time throughout your Doxology Day reviewing the items. Ask yourself, "Why am I reluctant to offer thanks to God for _____?" In my experience, I have felt God challenge my interpretation of particular items I have listed. Our ingratitude may be shaped by our inability to accurately perceive a situation. For example, I doubt that Joseph was initially in an attitude of gratitude as a single adult in jail, falsely accused of attempting to seduce Potiphar's wife. But the Scripture reports, "the LORD was with him" in that place (Genesis 39:23). Yet, eventually Joseph was able to stir this incident into his gratitude "batter" and confess to his brothers, "Even though you intended to do harm to me, God intended it for good, in order to preserve a numerous people, as he is doing today" (Genesis 50:20).

So, the first run through—"I am *not* grateful for . . . the broken engagement"—may, in turn, in time, turn into something for which you can be grateful. It takes time for us to comprehend the prevenient grace of God.

Our "now" focus may not always be accurate.

A Litany of Thanksgiving

We often need something of a jump start. The following prayer from *The Book of Common Prayer* may be helpful.

Let us give thanks to God our Father for all his gifts so freely bestowed upon us.

For the beauty and wonder of your creation, in earth and sky and sea, [I] thank you, Lord.

For all that is gracious in the lives of men and women, revealing the image of Christ, *[I] thank you, Lord.*

For our daily food and drink, our homes and families, and our friends, *[I] thank you, Lord.*

For minds to think, and hearts to love, and hands to serve,
[I] thank you, Lord.

For health and strength to work, and leisure to rest and play, *[I] thank you, Lord.*

For the brave and courageous, who are patient in suffering
and faithful in adversity, *[I] thank you, Lord.*

For all valiant seekers after truth, liberty, and justice,
[I] thank you, Lord.

Above all, we give you thanks for the great mercies and promises given to us in Christ Jesus our Lord,

To him be praise and glory, with you, O Father, and the
Holy Spirit, now and for ever. Amen.[55]

 O God, You have given me so many wonderful things such as
_____ *and* _____

Now give me one more thing: a grateful heart. I offer up to you my core
un'grato. Remind me, Lord, of your many benefits I forget so easily. Amen.

46. Celebrating the Sabbath ● ● ● ● ● ● ● ● ● ● ● ● ● ● ● ● ● ●

Even God took a day off!

"Remember the Sabbath Day by keeping it holy."—*Exodus 20:8*

"Remember the Sabbath Day" is not just a suggestion—it is a commandment and a vital element in a rooted healthy spirituality.

"Let's suppose," the seminary professor said in a hushed tone, "that you pastor a large church and your secretary interrupts you. 'Pastor, there's a member of the congregation who says she *has* to talk to you immediately.' "

"What's it about?" the pastor demands.

"She says that one of your associates is breaking one of the Ten Commandments flagrantly and publicly. Everyone knows."

"Send her in!" the pastor responds.

God's creation is varied and vast. We should rejoice in every opportunity to view his handiwork. Remember that wherever we roam on the planet—no matter how distant from all that is familiar and comfortable—he is our constant companion, and he always speaks the language. When you think about it, who is better to share the ecstatic communion of oohs and ahhs with than the Artist himself? [57]

"Now," the professor asked the class, "What would you do if you were that pastor?"

"I would confront him and if he admitted it, I would fire him on the spot!" one classmate snapped. Several students nodded in agreement.

"Why?" the professor countered.

"I am not going to tolerate anyone on my staff committing adultery!"

"Who said anything about adultery? The associate was breaking another commandment, Remember the Sabbath Day."

The quiet in the room was disarming. But the professor was not finished. "Now, we are very sensitive to the commandment, 'Thou shall not commit adultery,' but very, *very* insensitive to the commandment to remember the Sabbath Day. Yet, *all* Scripture is given by inspiration."

It's easy to memorize the Ten Commandments and to make a fuss about having them on public school classroom walls, but quite another issue to observe *all* of them. A case could be made that the commandment to remember the Sabbath Day is one of the most brazenly violated.

In the fall, Sunday in America is about N.F.L. football, right? I have been amazed at the difference in attendance in churches with multiple Sunday morning services, when the "big" game starts at eleven.

Even for those of us who are not football addicts, Sunday is often about dashing from here to there, with little time for a breather. We drop into bed Sunday night thinking of what did not get done before the new week starts. But at least, we tipped our hat at God in the morning.

If God needed a day off, so do we. Yet, some readers are extremely uncomfortable, thinking I am about to whiz us back to the era when the Blue Laws closed almost everything on Sundays. No, I do not want to return to the legalism of my childhood when Sunday was definitely not a fun day for children.

This country runs twenty-four hours a day, seven days a week. For some of us, Sunday is a work day and/or the busiest day of the week. The Ten Commandments do not say that Sunday has to be the Sabbath but that you—a single adult—need a day of rest, a Sabbath. A time out. But, for many single adults, Sunday is the busiest day of the week:

- ☐ Sunday school or single adult fellowship
- ☐ a worship service
- ☐ a single adult brunch or other meal
- ☐ Sunday evening activity

- ☐ Sunday evening worship or small group
- ☐ committee or single adult council meeting
- ☐ Sunday night after-church fellowship

And in many churches one is definitely not "spiritual" if not present for the Sunday evening service.

I grew up in a family that insisted on the Sunday afternoon nap. Today a real nap or an easy-paced Sunday is a luxury—"places to go, people to see." For some Sunday is a catch-up day for all that we did not get done in the previous week, or a get ahead day for jump starting the next week. A day of relaxation? I wish!

For some single parents, Sunday is "exchange" day when the kids return from a weekend with the noncustodial parent. While the absence may offer a much needed breather, some always wonder about what emotional state the children will be in when they return. For many single parents, Sunday is a lonely day, especially after you have returned children to the other parent. The Sunday ache is always fresh. Widow/ers have described it as incredibly lonely, especially if their children are grown. Memories of meals shared around a big family table or with a spouse cloud the day.

For some, Sunday morning is the only morning of the week we can sleep late or sleep in. Sunday school! Says who? That could be one factor explaining the growing popularity of Saturday night "lite" worship experiences. If one is in a framework that spiritual disciplines are to be checked off, one casual hour on Saturday night, when you can just show up, leads to a, "Well, that takes care of that!" and leaves Sunday freer. On the other hand, Saturday night worship is important for those who work on Sunday morning.

My concern is that many single adults "do" Sunday in such a way that there is no Sabbath and no rest. Francis Asbury, a single adult, first Bishop of the Methodist Church in America, paradoxically expected his ministers to take a day of rest, generally on Monday, but did not take a day off himself. "Any sort of rest day," his biographer noted, "was very irregular with him."[59]

It is too easy to give lip service to the Sabbath. It's too easy to believe that the Sabbath is some relic from our agrarian past.

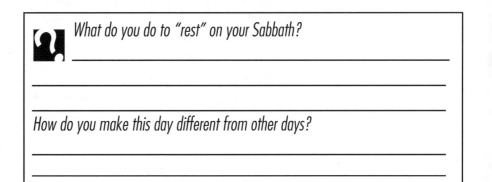

What do you do to "rest" on your Sabbath?

_____

_____

_____

How do you make this day different from other days?

_____

_____

One way to make the Sabbath more relaxed is to ask, "Do I really need to do this today? Will it wait?" To schedule some time to waste "well." Or as my friend Greg says, "to lie around and be lazy."

Tilden Edwards offers this model for Sabbath: I mean real Sabbath time, wherein one lets oneself simply *be* in prayer, jogging, reading, or other activity, with nothing whatsoever to produce, to make happen, to plan—even for oneself. For what purpose? Such times can help condition usually hard-driving and driven single adults to slow down and let their hearts sink effortlessly into the gospel. . . . We can afford to rest in such a divine Lover, whose living waters will refresh us if we still our crowded busyness for a while.[60]

Identify four ways you could "still" your crowded busyness and make room for a Sabbath.

1. _____
2. _____
3. _____
4. _____

Belle Bennett, a leading advocate for women in ministry in the then Methodist Episcopal Church South, practiced a strict Sunday observance. She would not open telegrams or special delivery letters on the Sabbath or even travel. One friend observed that Miss Bennett "suffered visible pain if long continental or worldwide travel necessitated her continuous going on the Sabbath Day." She believed that she needed the time for her soul to catch up with her body.[61]

"Sabbath time is meant to be an opportunity, not a burden." (Tilden Edwards) [62]

I am trying to make a Sabbath in my life, since I speak or preach on most Sundays. Surely speakers and writers are entitled to a day off—really off. So, often I take Wednesday and will attend a noon service at a cathedral. But I am struggling with this aspect of practicing the spiritual disciplines, especially when I am under pressure to finish a writing assignment. You may have to be creative in honoring the biblical command that begins with the word *remember*.

Invite God to influence your Sabbath-design.

Section 5

47. Making Space for God •••••••••••••••••••••

The opportunity for spiritual growth begins when we remove the "Do Not Disturb!" sign from our souls and make space for God.

"But I have calmed and quieted my soul."
—*Psalm 131:2*

Christmas week was too packed, but I knew that I wanted to make it to the Nelson Museum to see the Caravaggio and Tanzio exhibit on John the Baptist. In their time period, when most people could not read, religious art and stained-glass windows were two ways of gaining insight into faith. I marveled at the moodiness of John, the single adult who "prepared the way" for the coming of Christ. Caravaggio captured John in a less than happy mood. I needed to be reminded that saints are not always fun people to be around—after all, in many cases their convictions can cost them their lives.

Many of my Fundamentalist single adult friends would scoff at the idea of going to an art museum as a spiritual exercise. Yet, that's precisely what it was for me. I do not have the courage that John the Baptist had—to face down Herod. But his life, as seen in these paintings, reminds me that the call to obedience—radical obedience—is rooted in practicing the spiritual disciplines.

Sometimes we imagine that the people of the Bible are of colossal proportions, unimaginably spiritual. God gave [John the Baptist] an immense task. God gives everyone immense tasks. The chief thing to see is that God does not choose us because of our brilliance, or our piety, or our unwavering faithfulness. God chooses us because God wants us, in all the modesty of our gifts and abilities. God takes us as we are, living our workaday lives, and asks great things of us.[1]

Think back over the past month. How have you "wasted time well" or "made space for God"?

I _____.

I _____.

I _____.

Can you think of a leisure moment that you missed?

_____

_____

_____

I wandered down to the museum gift shop and soon found myself laughing. A group of creative artists had taken several famous paintings and slightly altered them with Christmas motifs. In the middle of a Maxfield Parrish masterpiece, I found Narcissus contemplating on a rock but wearing a Santa hat.

My favorite was Michelangelo's famed picture from the ceiling of the Sistine Chapel—the hand of God reaching out to the hand of Adam. In this "edited" print by Joo Chung, God was offering Adam a beautiful wrapped package. I bought the card and look at it from time to time, for it captures what I believe the quest for spirituality is all about: receiving the gift of God in Jesus Christ. Yet, many of us are content to admire the wrapping and never get into the present. Early that morning I had read moving words from a devotional book:

> Christmas comes and brings to us the greatest reassurance in the universe, which is that at the heart of the universe is the Someone whose principal activity is loving us, who meets us in the Bethlehem child—Emmanuel, God with us.[2]

By making space in the early moments of that Saturday, by reflecting on the words of the devotional, I was already "preparing the way" or making space for the experience in the gallery but also in the gift shop. Making space.

My colleague-mentor, Steve Harper, calls an experience like mine at the Nelson "wasting time well." I think of it as "spacing" or making space in my life and schedule for God's ambushes. Being willing to be interrupted. That is true leisure.

The words of a Christmas carol written by two single adults, Isaac Watts and George Frideric Handel, capture the essence of spacing in a phrase in "Joy to the World!"

> "Let every heart prepare Him room."
> (Isaac Watts) [3]

Watts didn't say, "Let the spiritual person prepare him room" but "Let *every heart*." The single adult must prepare room for God in the frail terrain of the soul.

> "We must be ready to allow ourselves to be interrupted by God. God will be constantly crossing our paths and canceling our plans . . . [by sending us people with claims and petitions]." (Dietrich Bonhoeffer) [4]

After his romantic wounds, only a deliberate spacing in Watts's life made room for spirituality that in turn made room for his great gift to the world: his hymn texts.

Single adults can become "wonders of his love" if we make space for him. I walked into friends' home on Christmas Day and immediately recognized the family room had been changed. When I commented, Beulah replied, "We had to rearrange everything to make space for the tree . . . it's so big." They could have had a small tree, but my friends made space for a big one. Saint Augustine in his *Confessions* pleaded, "Narrow is the mansion of my soul; enlarge Thou it, that Thou mayest enter in."[5] Spirituality is making room for God. We make space for God. This reality is captured by a single parent in this prayer.

"How wonderfully you fit, Lord in the rhythms of my life, now that I walk with you daily now that I sit quietly holding your hand reading your Psalms. Now that I caress my children and share with them the joy of your love, the peace of your words, how wonderfully you fit, Lord, in the rhythms of my life." (Ginger Farry) [6]

Can you say, "How wonderfully you fit, Lord . . ."?
☐ yes   ☐ no   ☐ unsure

What would it take to make more space in your life for God "to wonderfully fit"?

It would take _____.

It would take _____.

Complete the prayer: Lord, I want you to "wonderfully fit" in the rhythms of my life.

_____

_____

_____.

Amen.

48. Making Space for Worship • • • • • • • • • • • • • • • • •

The way I spent my life is the way I tell the world what I value.

". . . not neglecting to meet together, as is the habit of some." —*Hebrews 10:25*

"The physical presence of other Christians is a source of incomparable joy and strength to the believer. The believer feels no shame, as though he were still living too much in the flesh, when he yearns for the physical presence of other Christians." (Dietrich Bonhoeffer) [7]

Many single adults have difficulty finding a worship community that will fully accept them as single adults. In an era when churches are using family as part of their marketing strategy, many single adults feel out of place. They question if there is room in the pew for them. Divorced individuals feel this so clearly; many say it would be simpler if they wore a scarlet "D." Many widowed people say that church reminds them of their changed marital status. "We were part of the in-group in this church for twenty-five years!" One widow told me, "I just can't go to church alone."

Yet, we also live in an era of "spectator" worship.

"Among too many of the citizens the spirit of politics has, in whole or in part, eaten out the spirit of religion." (Francis Asbury) [8]

While I was in medical school, I became disenchanted with all such concepts, what I understood religious thought to be. Ironically, it was my experiences as a doctor at the bedsides of dying children that later led me to reconsider a Christian faith profession. It was children who were dying who invited me to enter their covenant, to attend a marriage feast.

My youthful experience of Christianity left me so skeptical about most churches that I inclined toward a do-it-yourself, designer religion. Organized religion seemed highly imperfect to me. I had my own cathedral, acres of virginal woods. I could read the Bible by myself, thank you, and commune with God in private. But it's hard to read that Book without looking for someone with whom its message can be shared. It's like attending a great performance alone and having no one to jab in the ribs when you get caught up in the ecstasy.

[Eventually] this lone gunslinger joined a local family of faith, imperfect as it may be, imperfect as I am. This faith family has been my sounding board as I continue to seek to integrate my growing faith in my life's work. This is what covenant is all about: uniting with others, extending the invitation, preparing for a feast. It's no fun to dine alone. [11]

The Church of What's Happening! will leave you spiritually breathless after sixty-action-packed minutes of "praise." All you have to do is show up, hope you can find a parking space and a seat, and sit back and "enjoy." It's show time. Ministers of music perform like friendly emcees. Church is a place where you can feel good without any of those uncomfortable topics disturbing the audience. And when you like something, applaud. Why, worship can be fun, these days, if you pick the right worship venue.

I am troubled by the "showbiz," feel-good approach to worship. I understand why some of my single friends are dropping out, especially those who have attended churches where one is more likely to hear a modified "Contract with America" than the gospel.

In some settings, worship includes a diatribe against someone who is "not like us" or "those people." I have been stunned by many women friends who have been wounded by the church and are part of a growing number of adults, single and married, who could be called "churchless believers." One "burned" church dropout said, "Jesus, I believe in. The church, no way!"

Yet, I also listen to people who have written extensively on spirituality, like Maxie Dunnam who insists, "There is no Christianity apart from the Church. This is true because there is no such thing as solitary Christianity."[9] Steve Harper adds that John Wesley—as a single and later as a husband and widower was "a churchman." He was not blind or out of touch with the imperfections of the church.

He did not do these things because he believed the Church of England was a pure or perfect church. He did not remain faithful to the Anglican Church because he felt its principles were beyond question. He did not remain an Anglican because everyone in the church believed the way he did. Wesley maintained his churchmanship for one reason: He knew that to be a Christian is to be an active member of the body of Christ. No one can be a Christian in isolation. Wesley's devotional life reminds us that there is no authentic spirituality apart from the church. God has called us to be in fellowship with the rest of

Take a moment to reread Harper's words on Wesley. Remember, Wesley remained unmarried [and wanted his preachers unmarried] until long after he founded the Methodist movement. What does his example say to you about participation in church worship?

the people of God. Our devotional life should motivate us toward that kind of support for one another, not away from it. . . . Wesley would tell us to beware of any devotional life that does not enrich our love for the church.[10]

Because of work schedules, some may be unable to attend a Sunday service, but can they find a community of faith with a weekday service? I often go downtown to Grace and Holy Trinity Cathedral to take part in the Wednesday noon service. Oh, I miss the music of Sunday worship, but it is still making a deliberate "space" for the holy in my life and in my week.

Another benefit of using *The Book of Common Prayer* is the worship rituals, for individuals or groups, for morning, noon, evening. Francis Asbury followed these exercises as he rode the circuits of early Methodism on horseback.

Sometimes, we have to move on from a familiar place of worship because it no longer meets our needs. I do not mean this in some egoist way: *my* needs. For example I grew up in a very nonliturgical faith community. However, that style of worship is not spiritually nurturing for me today. People who know my background, and who know that I am an Episcopalian, often say something like, "That's quite a leap." I respond, "No, that's a pilgrimage!"

As a single adult I need a worship community that
- [ ] remembers God as Father, Son, and Holy Spirit.
- [ ] rehearses God's mighty acts in history.
- [ ] celebrates the resurrection of Jesus Christ.
- [ ] takes discipleship seriously.
- [ ] makes time in worship for silence and for the confession of sin
- [ ] welcomes, not excludes.
- [ ] realizes that not all in attendance are married with 2.3 children, an IRA, and a boat in the driveway.
- [ ] is participant-oriented rather than spectator-oriented.
- [ ] acknowledges the historical worship traditions of the Christian faith, especially Eucharist.
- [ ] translates the extravagantly outrageous grace of Jesus into the daily lives of the congregation.
- [ ] models grace.

Sometimes we must "move on" from a particular worship community or tradition.

> Look over my list in the text and put a check mark by those that are essential for you. Or take some time and think about how you would prioritize this list. Perhaps there are other items you see as essential. For example, single parents may want a strong Christian education program for their children or a strong single adult ministry. In the space below add your priorities: The church I want to worship in will:
>
> _____
> _____

The Scripture reminds us that 2,000 years ago, as well as today, some people were not making "space" for worship in a community of faith. Worship is more than participating in a Bible study. Taking your spirituality seriously could cause you to reprioritize your work or career so that you can be an active participant in a community of believers.

> "Christian brotherhood is not an ideal which we must realize; it is, rather, a reality created by God in Christ in which we may participate."
> (Dietrich Bonhoeffer) [12]

> How do you participate in a community of faith?
>
> By _____
> By _____
> By _____
> By _____
> By _____
> By _____
> By _____
> By _____
> By _____

49. Making Space for Eucharist ● ● ● ● ● ● ● ● ● ● ● ● ● ● ● ●

This is great news: A single adult is inviting us to His table. All he asks is that we remember Him.

"Do this, as often as you drink it, in remembrance of me." —1 Corinthians 11:25

Eucharist. Communion. The Lord's Supper. By whatever name, one of the great distinctives of the Christian faith. And, these days, often a battleground. In my community of faith, the ministers announce that this is "*the Lord's* table" and therefore "open to *all* baptized Christians." But I have been in churches where it was open only to members of that church. I have served on planning committees for several large gatherings of single adult ministers and leaders and there has never been a Communion service because of all the residues of denominational tradition. We can't agree on how to observe it. What a tragedy! We are all committed to ministering to single adults, yet we could not gather around a common table and remember the greatest single adult who has ever lived. How that must grieve Jesus!

For a long time after my divorce, I had a difficult time taking Communion because I thought I was permanently unworthy. I grew up in a tradition that skipped most of the biblical teaching on Communion to focus on one verse, "Wherefore whosoever shall eat this bread, and drink this cup of the Lord, unworthily, shall be guilty of the body and blood of the Lord" (1 Corinthians 11:27).

Following St. Paul's instructions, you have examined yourself, and truly you are not presuming to come trusting in your own merits, for you are unworthy, and you know it. Take time to realize this and never let the phrase be mere words, but always the sincere expression of your own conviction. *The unworthy are welcomed at His table, but there is no place for the presumptuous there.* The Savior's forgiveness has been asked and received, but be watchful lest any pride, jealousy, or lack of love stand between you and another disciple [italics mine].[13]

My friend Jerry Hull helped me with his simple observation, "The only ones who are unworthy of communion are those who think they are worthy of it!" Steve Harper agrees: "Who is ever worthy? The sacrament is precisely for the unworthy, and that is all of us! We are sinners saved by grace. We approach Holy Communion as a means of grace, because it is a grace that we need."[14] Harper goes on to contend:

The problem of unworthiness resides in the way the sacrament is conducted, not in the character of those who partake. . . . Participation in the Lord's Supper is a step of obedience, not a sign of moral perfection. . . . The Lord's Supper is designed for those of us who know how much we need God![15]

How often do you take Communion?

_____ never   _____ monthly
_____ occasionally   _____ weekly

What shapes your attitude toward Communion?
_____ my denominational teaching
_____ the church I currently attend
_____ my family upbringing
_____ my personal faith

What is the most meaningful Communion service or Eucharist that you can remember? What made it so?

_____

_____

Summarize your attitude toward Communion:

_____

_____

I wish these words had been in print when I was first divorced. I think of all the spiritual sustenance I missed out on. In the Anglican tradition, we believe there are three benefits from regularly taking part in the Lord's Supper:

1. The forgiveness of sins (based on the confession of sin before partaking of the elements);
2. The strengthening of union with Christ and one another; and
3. The foretaste of the heavenly banquet (that will be presided over by a single adult).

There is one thing that annoys me about Communion: the practice of taking the cup in small slightly-larger-than-a-thimble plastic disposable cups. I really need a "big gulp!"—the forty-four ouncer. That little cup, I think, is a tip-off to a hidden callousness to the mystery of Communion: I don't need very much, thank you. I keep thinking of the Brylcream commercial, "a little dab will do ya'!" As a single adult, I need more than a thimbleful and how come no one ever goes back for seconds? Every great meal or banquet I have attended, the host has declared, "There's plenty. Who wants seconds?"

Never rise and leave this most sacred service without a look back to the Cross of Calvary, and without reminding yourself that Christ is risen, that He is alive, that you are remembering a living, not a dead Lord, and that He has promised to come again.[16]

Eucharist is a feast of memories and a pledge of reunion. Beyond this it means to each disciple exactly what he has insight to discern and faith to comprehend.[17]

Before the elements are served, I so appreciate hearing these words after the consecration of the elements: *"The gifts of God for the People of God,"* and the wonderful reassuring words that follow: "Take them in remembrance that Christ died for you, and feed on him in your hearts by faith, with thanksgiving."[18]

"To feed on him in your hearts" is to meditate, to contemplate the impact of his grace. That's why the Eucharist has to involve your brain as much as your mouth. A few times a year is not a sufficient enough reminder for me of the sacrifice Christ made to redeem me.

I suggest three things for single adults participating in Holy Communion:

☐ *that we examine our lives* [and sometimes we will need to hum: "Not my brother, not my sister, not my ex-spouse, O Lord, standing in the need of prayer . . .";

☐ *that we repent of our sins* (major league and minor); and

☐ *that we be in love and charity with all people (that may mean that we are working at it)*.[19]

> In this examination that leads to taking the bread and cup, I may need to ask God to help me have right attitudes:
>
> —toward an ex
> —toward the "third party" that broke up my marriage
> —toward those who took my ex's side
> —toward the person who broke up with me recently
> —of my resentfulness toward married friends
> —of the polite jealousy toward the seemingly "happy" families of others
> —toward those who are insensitive to the needs of single adults

We need to be reminded that if anyone understands our singleness it is Jesus. He knew, that generations in the future, some of us would struggle with feeling worthy of participating in the Eucharist. That's why I like to remind people that it is *"The Lord's Table"* and not _____'s table!

I am still overwhelmed that I cannot recite all of the closing prayer of the Eucharist with the congregation. The prayer opens, "Eternal God, heavenly Father, you have graciously accepted us as living members . . ."[20] which really means, you have graciously accepted *me*. What a word: *graciously*. Not reluctantly, not grudgingly, but graciously! Not into a country club or a museum of the holy, but into a community of faith. Often that reality brings a lump in my throat and tears to my eyes. I have found myself unable to keep up with the congregation's recitation. I am still savoring that word *graciously*. The mystery of acceptance is still overpowering. I hope I never get comfortable with that prayer.

The Eucharist prayer closes:

Send us now into the world in peace, and grant strength and courage to love and serve you with gladness and singleness of heart.[21]

"We become who we are meant to be by becoming the receptive, strong, serene, and capable persons God has called us to be from the beginning." (Susan Muto)[22]

Thus, through the Eucharistic meal we gain the "strength and courage to love and serve" God in our single season, however long it lasts. I want this to be a celebration in anticipation of God's great table in heaven—in anticipation of that great day when there will be plenty of room for all of God's children!

50. Making the Choices for Spirituality • • • • • • • • • • •

Spirituality is a pilgrimage, reinforced by choices.

"But as for me and my household, we will serve the Lord."—*Joshua 25:15*

As a child, I loved to sing, "You take the high road, and I'll take the low road, and I'll be in Scotland before you." In my spiritual pilgrimage I have learned that there are high roads and there are low paths to spirituality.

In the moments when I give in to my sweet tooth and buy candy, I often buy a third or quarter pound, rationalizing that there are not as many calories that way. Some single adults want about "a quarter pound of God." Definitely not too much, or they could be mistaken for "holy rollers." Others want religious vaccinations—a brief exposure to God.

The single season, whether intentional or not, is an incredible opportunity to venture deep into the inner spaces of our beings. I like the way my artist friend Joy Wallace said it:

> I think we all need a private corner (even if it's just a corner of our minds!), a simple, solitary quietude, where our dreams can come out and play . . . where the distinction between "reality" and imagination blurs. Peace lives there. Make yourself at home. You are![23]

"You shall love the Lord your God with all your heart, and with all your soul, and with all your mind. This is the greatest commandment and first."—*Matthew 22:37-38*

All includes our imagination. The psalmist insisted, "Bless the LORD, O my soul: and all that is within me, bless his holy name" (Psalm 103:1, KJV). "All that is within me," is "all that is me." Spirituality is a balance of heart, soul, and mind, although in some seasons of our lives, one of those elements may dominate.

"[Spirituality] is not a private possession granted to select souls but a universal call issued to each of us." (Susan Muto) [24]

For when I go back to Joo Chung's modification of Michelangelo, I see that the package in God's hand, has my name on it, and yours.

Although we have come to the end of our time together, we will never end our quest for spirituality. It is a journey, not a destination. Daily, hourly, there are new lessons, new experiences, new reminders of grace. It is a decision as Joshua would remind us. As for me, I will serve the Lord.

No wonder Isaac Watts could proclaim, "Joy to the World, the Lord is come . . . Let every heart prepare him room." Perhaps after this time of reflecting, reading, thinking, journaling, wondering, you need to compose a final prayer, remembering the four elements of prayer: adoration, confession, thanksgiving, and supplication.

A Prayer of Examination

Prayer of Adoration:

_____

_____

_____

Prayer of Confession:

_____

_____

_____

Prayer of Thanksgiving:

_____

_____

_____

Prayer of Supplication:
[Perhaps you want to ask God to help you with some of the particular disciplines
detailed in this book. Perhaps you want to explore them and invite God's help.
Make this part of your supplication.]

_____

_____

_____

AMEN.

Spirituality is not something that just happens. You make choices, decisions, investments of time, choices to pray, "God, help me to take you seriously." There are no experts; we are all beginners. Over 200 years ago, a single adult who dared to take God seriously, prayed, "Lord, keep me watchful." Francis Asbury founded the Methodist Church in America. Could God be wanting to do his next big project through you? If so, it will be because you are spiritually prepared and watchful.

"Rose up this morning with a determination to fight or die; and spent an hour in earnest prayer. Lord, keep me watchful." (Francis Asbury) [25]

"Lord, keep me watchful."

_____ *Signed*

_____ *date*

Who's Who of Quoted Single Adults

Asbury, Francis (1745–1816), first Bishop of the Methodist Church in America, father of American Methodism.

Bennett, Belle (1852–1922), founder of Scarritt College and major leader for recognition of full ministry for women in the Methodist Church.

Berry, Martha (1866–1942), founder of Berry College in Rome, Georgia, Presbyterian layperson.

Blair, Martha (1954–), freelance writer and single parent.

Bonhoeffer, Dietrich (1906–1945), Lutheran pastor and theologian, executed by the Nazis.

Brainerd, David (1718–1747), missionary to American Indians.

Brooks, Phillips (1835–1893), theologian, Episcopal Bishop of Massachusetts, wrote "O Little Town of Bethlehem."

Buzick, Ilona (1951–), pastor of Roanoke Presbyterian Church in Kansas City, and director, Presbyterians in Prayer.

Cable, Mildred (1877–1952), and Francesca French (no dates available) were missionaries in the Shansi Province of China and established one of the first schools for girls in China.

Carmichael, Amy (1867–1951), founder of the Dohnavur Fellowship in India, and developed orphanage care system.

Carver, George Washington (1864–1943), researcher at Tuskegee Institution who developed hundreds of uses for the peanut.

Dickinson, Emily (1839–1886), American poet, wrote over 1,700 poems.

Dix, Dorothea (1802–1887), reformer and humanitarian, headed nursing efforts during the Civil War.

Dobbels, William J. (1948–1990), Jungian psychologist and author of *An Epistle of Comfort*.

Dysart, Stella (1878–1966), miner, Presbyterian philanthropist.

Edwards, Tilden (1935–), director of the Salem Institute in Washington, D.C., recognized as one of the leaders in contemporary spiritual formation.

Elliott, Charlotte (1789–1871), English poet, best known for the words to the hymn, "Just As I Am."

Farry, Ginger (1941–), lecturer on spirituality, single parent, author of *The Divorced Woman's Prayerbook*.

Glaser, Chris (1951–), lecturer, author, and AIDS activist.

Hale, Sarah Josepha (1788–1879), widow, editor of *Godey's Magazine*, and lobbyist for American Thanksgiving as official holiday.

Hammarskjöld, Dag (1905–1961), career Swedish diplomat, Secretary General of the United Nations, 1953–1961, winner of the Nobel Peace Prize.

Harkness, Georgia (1891–1974), Methodist theologian, author of thirty-eight books.

Havergal, Francis (1836–1879), wrote more than one hundred hymns, known best for "Take My Life, and Let It Be."

Huebsch, Bill (1951–), Catholic lay theologian and author.

Keller, Helen (1880–1968), humanitarian and activist for the visually impaired, challenged public awareness of the needs of the disabled.

Kierkegaard, Søren (1813–1855), Danish religious writer and philosopher.

Koob, Kathryn (1938–), state department official in Iran, held as hostage 1979–1981.

Lewis, C. S. (1898–1963), English poet, Oxford don, single adult who married American single parent, known for *The Chronicles of Narnia* and his experience as a widower, *A Grief Observed*.

McAllaster, Elva (1922–), author of *Free to Be Single*, poet in residence, Greenville College.

McCheyne, Robert Murray (1813–1843), Church of Scotland pastor.

Marshall, Catherine, widow, single parent.

Mears, Henrietta (1890–1961), served as Director of Christian Education at Hollywood Presbyterian Church for three decades, founder of Gospel Light Publishers, spiritual influence on Billy Graham.

Muto, Susan (1945–), Catholic lay theologian and director of Epiphany Associates, major author on spirituality.

Nightingale, Florence (1820–1910), nursing innovator and humanitarian.

Price, Eugenia (1916–1996), American novelist and writer on spirituality.

Ramsey, Evelyn (1933–1989), missionary physician in Africa and New Guinea, translator, author.

Rand, Roberta (1945–) is a freelance writer specializing in single adult issues. She wrote *Playing the Tuba at Midnight: The Joys and Challenges of Singleness*.

Rossetti, Christina (1830–1894), English poet and lyricist, emphasized religious themes.

Simeon, Charles (1759–1836), Church of England reformer, pastor Church of the Holy Trinity in Cambridge for more than five decades.

Stanley, Sir Henry (1841–1904), journalist and explorer, known for finding Dr. David Livingstone in Central African jungle.

Streeter, Carole Sanderson (1935–), former missionary, author on spirituality, single parent.

Ten Boom, Corrie (1891–1893), survived German camps in World War II, became an evangelist, known for her experience of hiding Jewish people in the Netherlands.

Thrasher, Lillian (1887–1961), founder of orphanage in Egypt.

Warner, Anna (1824–1915), novelist, Bible teacher at West Post, wrote chorus, "Jesus Loves Me This I Know."

Warner, Susan (1819–1885), novelist, who with her sister wrote more than eighty-five novels, short stories, and biographies.

Watts, Isaac (1674–1748), father of English hymnology, composed over 700 hymns.

White, Eartha Mary Magdalene, (1876–1975), social worker in Jacksonville, Florida.

Williams, Robin (1951–), Assemblies of God clergy person, author.

Holy! Me?

Notes

Section 1

1. Susan Annette Muto, *Pathways of Spiritual Living* (Garden City, N.Y.: Doubleday, 1984), p. 141.

2. Ibid., p. 25.

3. Susan Annette Muto, *Celebrating the Single Life: A Spirituality for Single Persons in Today's World* (Garden City, N.Y.: Doubleday, 1982), p. 49.

4. Charlotte Elliott, "Just As I Am," *Worship in Song Hymnal* (Kansas City: Lillenas Publishing, 1972), p. 232.

5. *The Book of Common Prayer* (New York: Seabury, 1979), p. 323.

6. Carole Sanderson Streeter, *Reflections for Women Alone* (Wheaton, Ill.: Victor Books, 1987), p. 19.

7. Muto, *Pathways*, p. 25.

8. William D. Longstaff, "Take Time to Be Holy," *Worship in Song Hymnal* (Kansas City: Lillenas Publishing, 1972), p. 33.

9. Muto, *Pathways*, p. 96.

10. William Josef Dobbels, *An Epistle of Comfort* (Kansas City: Sheed and Ward, 1990), p. 7.

Section 2

1. Georgia Harkness, *The Providence of God* (Nashville: Abingdon Press, 1960).

2. Anna B. Warner, "Jesus Loves Me." *Worship in Song Hymnal* (Kansas City: Lillenas, 1972), p. 497.

3. Eleanor L. Doan, ed. *431 Quotes from the Notes of Henrietta C. Mears* (Glendale, Calif.: Gospel Light, 1961), p. 62.

4. John Stott, *Christian Basics: A Handbook of Beginnings, Beliefs and Behavior* (Grand Rapids: Baker, 1991), p. 116.

5. Henrietta C. Mears, *What the Bible Is All About* (Ventura, Calif.: Gospel Light, 1983), p. 20.

6. Stott, p. 118.

7. James Bryant Smith, *A Spiritual Formation Workbook* (San Francisco: Harper San Francisco, 1991), p. 38.

8. Steve Harper, *Devotional Life in the Wesleyan Tradition: A Workbook* (Nashville: Upper Room Books, 1995), p. 68.

9. Ibid., p. 70.

10. Harold Ivan Smith, *Movers and Shapers: Singles Who Changed Their World* (Old Tappan, N.J.: Revell, 1988), p. 179.

11. Harper, p. 66.

12. Susan Annette Muto, *Celebrating the Single Life: A Spirituality for Single Persons in Today's World* (Garden City, N.Y.: Doubleday, 1982), p. 135.

13. Dietrich Bonhoeffer, *Life Together.* Translated by John W. Doberstein (New York: Harper Bros. 1954), pp. 56-57.

14. Corrie ten Boom, *Amazing Love* (Fort Washington, Pa.: Christian Literature Crusade, 1953), p. 32.

15. Stott, p. 117.

16. Ethel May Baldwin and David V. Benson, *Henrietta Mears and How She Did It* (Ventura, Calif.: Regal, 1966), p. 38.

17. Muto, *Celebrating*, p. 135.

18. Susan Annette Muto, *Pathways of Spiritual Living* (Garden City, N.Y.: Doubleday, 1984), p. 67.

19. Robert M. Mulholland, *Shaped by the Word* (Nashville: Upper Room Books, 1985), pp. 49-58.

20. Barbara Hudson Powers, *The Henrietta Mears Story* (Old Tappan, N.J.: Fleming Revel, 1965), p. 58.

21. Earl C. Wolf, ed. *The Best of Bertha Munro: Memorial Edition* (Kansas City: Beacon Hill, 1987), p. 199.

22. Eugenia Price, *What Really Matters: What Is Truly Essential to Christian Life* (New York: Dial, 1983), p. 97.

23. Bill Wolfe, "How to Choose a Bible," *Louisville Courier-Journal* (December 4, 1995), p. C-11.

24. Priests for Equality, *The Inclusive New Testament* (W. Hyattsville, Md.: 1994), p. 40.

25. Rosemary Lea, *Miss Lea's Bible Stories for Children* (New York: Zagat Survey, 1994), pp. 67-68.

26. Hugh Evan Hopkins, *Charles Simeon of Cambridge* (Grand Rapids: Eerdmans, 1977), p. 57.

27. Michael E. Williams, ed., *The Storyteller's Companion to the Bible: Judges–Kings*, vol. 3 (Nashville: Abingdon Press, 1992), p. 9.

28. Hopkins, p. 57.

29. Amy Carmichael, quoted in *The Gift of Prayer: A Treasury of Personal Prayer from the World's Traditions* (New York: Continuum, 1995), p. 72.

30. Bonhoeffer, p. 53.

31. Dietrich Bonhoeffer, *The Cost of Discipleship*, rev. ed. (New York: Macmillan, 1963), p. 37.

32. Ibid., p. 250.

33. Ibid., p. 47.

34. Paul Little, cited in Harper, p. 74.

35. Gerna Lerner, *The Grimke Sisters from South Carolina* (New York: Schocken Books, 1967), p. 139.

36. Wolfe, p. 33.

37. Bonhoeffer, *Life Together*, pp. 56-57.

38. Mulholland, p. 115.

39. Megan McKenna, *Not Counting Women and Children: Neglected Stories from the Bible* (Maryknoll: Orbis Books, 1994), p. 225.

40. Eugene Peterson, *The Message: The New Testament in Contemporary English* (Colorado Springs: Navpress, 1993), pp. 180-81.

41. Martin L. Smith, *The Word Is Very Near You: A Guide to Praying with Scripture* (Cambridge, Mass.: Cowley, 1989), pp. 105-07.

42. Mulholland, p. 114.

43. Basil Pennington, *The Way Back Home: An Introduction to Centering Prayer* (New York: Paulist, 1989), p. 28.

44. Una Roberts Lawrence, *Lottie Moon* (Nashville: Sunday School Board of the Southern Baptist Convention), p. 127, 67.

45. Pennington, p. 28.

46. Stott, p. 110.

47. Pennington, p. 28.

48. L. C. Rudolph, *Francis Asbury* (Nashville: Abingdon Press, 1966), p. 141.

49. Muto, *Pathways*, p. 74.

50. Harold Ivan Smith, *Movers and Shapers*, p. 105.

51. Rudolph, p. 141.

52. See "Phillips Brooks" in Harold Ivan Smith, *Movers and Shapers*, pp. 32-50.

53. Elisabeth Elliot, *A Chance to Die: The Life and Legend of Amy Carmichael* (Old Tappan, N.J.: Fleming Revell, 1987), p. 315.

54. Rudolph, p. 123.

55. Malu Halasa, *Mary McLeod Bethune* in series, *Black Americans of Achievement* (New York: Chelsea House, 1989), p. 24; Archives, Bethune-Cookman College, Daytona Beach, Florida.

56. Elton Trueblood, essay in *The Courage to Grow Old*, Phillip L. Berman, ed. (New York: Ballentine, 1989), p. 295.

57. Eugenia Price, *Diary of a Novel* (New York: Lippincott and Crowell, 1980), p. 46.

58. L. David Duff, *The Ramsey Covenant: A Story About Evelyn Ramsey, M.D.* (Kansas City: Nazarene Publishing House, 1985), p. 29.

59. Corrie ten Boom, *Tramp for the Lord* (Fort Washington, Pa.: Christian Literature Crusade, 1974), p. 130.

60. Ibid., p. 128.

61. C. S. Lewis, *Letters to Malcolm: Chiefly on Prayer* (New York: Harcourt, Brace & World, 1964), p. 90.

62. Doan, p. 62.

Section 3

1. Robert Murray McCheyne quoted in Sherwood Eliot Wirt and Kersten Beckstrom, *Topical Encyclopedia of Living Quotations* (Minneapolis: Bethany House, 1982), p. 177.

2. Corrie ten Boom with C. C. Carlson, *In Father's House* (Old Tappan, N.J.: Power Books, 1976), p. 26.

3. Susan Muto, *Pathways of Spiritual Living* (Garden City, N.Y.: Doubleday, 1984), p. 122.

4. C. S. Lewis, *Letters to Malcolm: Chiefly on Prayer* (New York: Harcourt, Brace & World, 1964), p. 19.

5. Joseph M. Scriven, "What a Friend We Have in Jesus," *Worship in Song Hymnal* (Kansas City: Lillenas, 1972), p. 123.

6. Ethel May Baldwin and David V. Benson, *Henrietta Mears and How She Did It* (Ventura, Calif.: Regal, 1966), p. 175.

7. John Friel, *Rescuing Your Spirit* (Deerfield Beach, Fla.: Health Communications, 1993), p. 161.

8. Kathleen White, *Amy Carmichael* (Minneapolis: Bethany House, 1986), pp. 110-11.

9. Dag Hammarskjöld, *Markings*, trans. Leif Sjoberg and W. H. Auden (New York: Knopf, 1965), p. 142.

10. Merle Armitage, *Stella Dysart of Ambrosia Lake* (New York: Dwell, Sloane & Pearce, 1959), p. 161.

11. Eugene Peterson, *The Message: The New Testament in Contemporary English* (Colorado Springs: Navpress, 1993), p. 146.

12. Priests for Equality, *The Inclusive New Testament* (W. Hyattsville, Md., 1994), p. 120.

13. Mary Christine DeBardeleben, *Lambuth-Bennett Book of Remembrance* (Nashville: Publishing House of the Methodist Episcopal Church, South, 1922), p. 305.

14. Dietrich Bonhoeffer, *Meditating on the Word*, David McI. Gracie, ed. (Nashville, Upper Room Books/Cowley Press, 1986), p. 62.

15. McCheyne, *Topical Encyclopedia of Living Quotations*, p. 182.

16. Muto, *Pathways*, p. 154.

17. Bonhoeffer, *Meditating*, p. 60.

18. Arnold Lobel, *Days with Toads and Frog* (New York: Harper & Row, 1979), p. 64.

19. Søren Kierkegaard, *The Oxford Book of Prayer* (New York: Oxford University Press, 1985), p. 146.

20. Amy Carmichael, *Topical Encyclopedia of Living Quotations*, p. 178.

21. Hammarskjöld, p. 83.

22. Muto, *Pathways*, p. 54.

23. Memorial service for Corrie ten Boom, April 22, 1983, Santa Ana, California, printed by Fleming H. Revell, 1983.

24. *The Book of Common Prayer* (New York: Seabury, 1979), p. 323.

25. Lillian Thrasher Papers, Archives, The Assembly of God International Offices, Springfield, Missouri.

26. Isaac Watts, *Aids to Devotions*, 2nd ed. (Boston: Lincoln and Edmands, 1832), p. 133.

27. Ibid.

28. *The Book of Common Prayer*, p. 320.

29. Ibid., p. 268.

30. Dietrich Bonhoeffer, *Life Together*, trans. John W. Doberstein (New York: Harper Bros, 1954), p. 29.

31. Søren Kierkegaard, p. 65.

32. Memorial Service for Corrie ten Boom.

33. Christina Rossetti, *Topical Encyclopedia of Living Quotations*, p. 239.

34. Helen Keller, *Topical Encyclopedia of Living Quotations*, p. 239.

35. Desmond Tutu, *An African Prayer Book* (New York: Doubleday, 1995), p. 63.

36. William J. Dobbels, *An Epistle of Comfort* (Kansas City: Sneed & Ward, 1990), p. 111.

37. Bonhoeffer, *Meditations*, p. 51.

38. Harold Ivan Smith, "Intercessors Follow Through on Offerings of Prayer," *Saint Andrews* 50:6 (February 11, 1996), pp. 1-2.

39. Dietrich Bonhoeffer, *Letters and Papers from Prison*, rev. ed., Eberhard Bethge, ed. (New York: Macmillan, 1967), p. 101.

40. Carole C. Carson, *Corrie ten Boom: Her Life, Her Faith* (Old Tappan, N.J.: Revell, 1983), p. 16.

41. Mrs. Jesse Lee Cunninggim, "A Brief Review of the Life of Belle Harris Bennett," Founder's Day Ceremonies, Scarritt College, Nashville, Tennessee, May 15, 1952, 16.

42. Armitage, p. 25.

43. Ilona Buzick, *Roanoke Presbyterian Church News*, Kansas City, Missouri, August 5, 1992.

44. Paris Donehoo, *Prayer in the Life of Jesus* (Nashville: Broadman, 1984), pp. 12-13.

45. Watts, p. 84.

46. Corrie ten Boom with John and Elizabeth Sherrill, *The Hiding Place* (Old Tappan, N.J.: Spire Books/Revell, 1971), pp. 43-45.

47. Ibid., p. 44.

48. Ibid., p. 45.

49. Walter Erdman, *Sources of Power in Famous Lives* (New York: Cokesbury, 1939), p. 140.

50. *The Book of Common Prayer*, pp. 832-33.

51. Pat Windsor, "Father Thomas Keating Brings Contemplation Out of the Cloister." *St. Anthony Messenger*, February 1992, p. 15.

52. Donehoo, p. 7.

53. Windsor, p. 15.

54. Søren Kierkegaard quoted in Appleton, p. 259.

55. Tutu, xvii.

56. Charlotte Elliott, "Just As I Am," *The United Methodist Hymnal* (Nashville: The United Methodist Publishing House, 1989), no. 357.

57. Personal conversation with David Messenger, Corrie ten Boom's physician and friend.

58. John Spong, *The Easter Moment* (San Francisco: Harper & Row, 1980), p. 209.

59. Tutu, p. 118.

60. Muto, *Pathways*, p. 121.

61. Isaac Watts, "O God, Our Help in Ages Past," *Worship in Song Hymnal* (Kansas City: Lillenas, 1972), p. 14.

62. Francis Ridley Havergal, "Take My Life, and Let It Be," *The United Methodist Hymnal* (Nashville: The United Methodist Publishing House, 1989), no. 399.

63. Donehoo, p. 8.

64. *Forward Day by Day*, v. 41. November–December 1995. January 1996, p. 25.

65. Muto, *Celebrating*, p. 132.

66. Chris Glaser, *The Word Is Out* (San Francisco: Harper San Francisco, 1994), September 19.

67. *The Book of Common Prayer*, p. 836.

68. Ibid., p. 827.

69. Bookmarker found at Canterbury Cathedral, Chapel of the Saints and Martyrs of Our Own Time.

70. Hammarskjöld, *Markings*, p. 100.

71. Ibid.

72. Corrie ten Boom in Connell, *Book of Prayers*, 64.

73. Kierkegaard, *Oxford Book of Prayer*, p. 79.

74. Kerrie Hide, *A Woman's Healing Song: Prayers of Consolation for the Separated and Divorced* (Mystic, Conn.: Twenty-Third Publications, 1993), pp. 22, 62.

75. James Weldon Johnson, "Lift Every Voice and Sing," *The United Methodist Hymnal* (Nashville: The United Methodist Publishing House, 1989), no. 519.

76. Ibid., no. 375.

77. *Saint Benedict's Prayer Book* (York, England: Ampleforth Abbey Press, 1993), p. 81.

78. Ibid., p. 62.

79. Tutu, xx.

80. *Forward Day by Day*, inside cover.

81. Thomas Merton, *Thoughts in Solitude* (New York: Farrar, Straus, & Giroux, 1956), p. 83.

82. Muto, *Pathways*, p. 121.

83. C. S. Lewis, *The Screwtape Letters* (New York: Macmillan, 1959).

84. Hammarskjöld, *Markings*, p. 89.

85. Muto, *Pathways*, p. 87.

Section 4

1. Susan Annette Muto, *Pathways of Spiritual Living* (Garden City, N.Y.: Doubleday, 1984), pp. 95-96.

2. Dag Hammarskjöld, *Markings*, trans. Leif Sjoberg and W. H. Auden (New York: Knopf, 1965), p. 205.

3. Muto, *Pathways*, p. 98.

4. Morton T. Kelsey, *Adventure Inward: Christian Growth Through Personal Journal Writing* (Minneapolis: Augsburg, 1980), p. 132.

5. Ibid., p. 46.

6. Frederick Buechner, *Telling Stories* (San Francisco: HarperCollins, 1991), p. 30.

7. Elmer T. Clark, Jacob S. Payton, J. Manning Potts, eds., *The Journals of Francis Asbury: The Journal 1771 to 1793*, vol. 1 (Nashville: Abingdon, 1958), xx.

8. Kathryn Kolb quoted in Ronald Klug, *How to Keep a Spiritual Journal: A Guide to Journal Keeping for Inner Growth and Personal Recovery* (Nashville: Thomas Nelson, 1982), p. 28.

9. Nathan Harms, "A Place to Be Your Soul," *Christian Single*, September 1995, pp. 44-45.

10. Klug, p. 58.

11. Harms, p. 45.

12. Ibid., p. 44.

13. Ibid.

14. Adapted from R. Benjamin Cirlin, "Saying Goodbye After Goodbye," presentation at National Hospice Conference on Bereavement, San Francisco, August 20, 1995.

15. Ben Campbell Johnson, *Pastoral Spirituality: A Focus for Ministry* (Philadelphia: Westminster, 1988), Appendix.

16. Klug, p. 58.

17. Muto, *Pathways*, p. 108.

18. Ibid., p. 106.

19. *Journals of Asbury*, xxi.

20. *Forward Day by Day*, v. 41. November–December 1995, January 1996, p. 46.

21. Gary R. Kremer, *George Washington Carver In His Own Words* (Columbia: Univ. Missouri Press, 1987), p. 137.

22. Joyce Blackburn, *Martha Berry: Little Woman with a Big Dream* (Philadelphia: Lippincott, 1968), p. 137.

23. Elva McAllaster, *Free to Be Single* (Chappaqua, N.Y.: Christian Herald Books, 1979), pp. 25-26.

24. Kremer, p. 135.

25. Ibid.

26. Ibid., p. 132.

27. Bill Huebsch, *A New Look at Prayer: Searching for Bliss* (Mystic, Conn.: Twenty-Third Publications, 1991), p. 79.

28. Corrie ten Boom, *Memorial Service Booklet.*

29. Emily Dickinson quoted in *Familiar Quotations*, 15th ed., Emily Morison Beck, ed. (Boston: Little, Brown & Co., 1980), 606:12.

30. Walter Russell Bowie, *Women of Distinction* (New York: Harper & Row, 1963), p. 89.

31. Lillian Thrasher, *Letters from Lillian*, (Springfield, Mo.: Assemblies of God, 1983), p. 114.

32. Susan Warner quoted in *The New Quotable Woman*, Elaine Partnow, ed., (New York: Facts on File, 1992), p. 189.

33. Eartha White quoted in *The Florida Times Union* (Jacksonville) November 13, 1966, 7.

34. Francis Borden, "Merry Christmas Seals," *American Way*, December 10, 1985, pp. 47-48.

35. Dorothea Dix in Partnow, p. 169.

36. Personal conversation with Father John Powell, S.J. on Feb. 5, 1997.

37. Eartha White Papers, Archives, University of North Florida, Jacksonville, Florida.

38. Richard A. Hasler, *Journey with David Brainerd* (Downer's Grove, Ill.: InterVarsity Press, 1975), p. 33.

39. Edward Everett Hale to Helen Keller quoted in *Familiar Quotations*, 590:5.

40. Winston Groom, *Gumpisms: The Wit and Wisdom of Forest Gump* (New York: Pocket Books, 1994), p. 88.

41. Alexander V. G. Allen, *Phillips Brooks: Memories of His Life with Extracts from His Letters and Notebooks* (New York: Dutton, 1907), p. 631.

42. Ethel May Baldwin and David V. Benson, *Henrietta Mears and How She Did It* (Ventura, Calif.: Regal, 1966), p. 83.

43. DeBardeleben, p. 89.

44. Sarah Josepha Hale quoted in Partnow, p. 151.

45. Huebsch, p. 40.

46. Helen Keller quoted in Partnow, p. 268.

47. Eartha White Papers, Archives.

48. Windsor, *Keating*, p. 13.

49. Ibid.

50. Huebsch, p. 40.

51. Blackburn, p. 105.

52. McAllaster, p. 278.

53. Martha Blair, *Lifewire*, First Church of the Nazarene, Salem, Oregon.

54. Watts, *Aids to Devotion*, p. 100.

55. *The Book of Common Prayer*, pp. 836-37.

56. Tilden Edwards, *Sabbath Time* (Nashville: Upper Room Books, 1992), p. 15.

57. Roberta Rand, *Playing the Tuba at Midnight* (Downer's Grove, Ill.: Inter-Varsity, 1995), p. 71.

58. Edwards, p.15.

59. Rudolph, p. 83.

60. Edwards, p. 136.

61. Carolyn L. Stapleton, "Belle Harris Bennett: Model of Holistic Christianity," *Methodist History*, 21 (April 1983), p. 131.

62. Edwards, p. 136.

Section 5

1. *Forward Day by Day*, v. 41. November–December 1995, January 1996, p. 43.

2. Ibid., p. 55.

3. Isaac Watts, "Joy to the World," *Sing to the Lord Hymnal* (Kansas City: Lillenas, 1993), p. 173.

4. Dietrich Bonhoeffer, *Life Together*, trans. John W. Doberstein (New York: Harper Bros. 1954), p. 99.

5. Augustine.

6. Ginger Farry, *The Divorced Woman's Prayerbook* (New York: Paulist, 1992), p. 47.

7. Bonhoeffer, *Life Together*, p. 19.

8. Elmer T. Clark, Jacob S. Payton, J. Manning Potts, eds., *The Journals of Francis Asbury: The Journal 1771 to 1793*, vol. 1 (Nashville: Abingdon, 1958), p. 413.

9. Maxie Dunnam, *This Is Christianity* (Nashville: Abingdon Press, 1994), p. 84.

10. Steve Harper, *Devotional Life in the Wesleyan Tradition: A Workbook* (Nashville: Upper Room Books, 1995), p. 35.

11. Diane Komp, *A Child Shall Lead Them: Lessons in Hope from Children with Cancer* (Grand Rapids: Zordervan, 1993), pp. 162–63.

12. Bonhoeffer, *Life Together*, p. 30.

13. Mildred Cable and Francesca French, *Toward Spiritual Maturity: A Book for Those Who Seek It* (London: Hodder & Straughton, 1973), p. 73.

14. Harper, p. 37.

15. Ibid.

16. Cable and French.

17. Ibid.

18. *The Book of Common Prayer*, p. 365.

19. Ibid., p. 860.

20. Ibid., p. 365.

21. Ibid., p. 366.

22. Susan Annette Muto, *Pathways of Spiritual Living* (Garden City, N.Y.: Doubleday, 1984), p. 167.

23. Correspondence with Joy Wallace.

24. Muto, *Pathways*, p. 171.

25. Asbury, *Journal*, p. 71.